BASHAN AND I

BASHAN AND I

THOMAS MANN

Translated by
Herman George Scheffauer

Pine St Books

Originally published 1923 Constable & Co. Ltd.
First Pine Street Books paperback edition published 2003

Printed in the United States of America on acid-free paper

10   9   8   7   6   5   4   3   2   1

Pine Street Books is an imprint of
University of Pennsylvania Press
Philadelphia, Pennsylvania 19104-4011

Library of Congress Cataloging-in-Publication Data

Mann, Thomas, 1875-1955
    Bashan and I / Thomas Mann ; translated by Herman George
Scheffauer

        p.   cm.
    ISBN 0-8122-1833-7 (pbk : alk. paper)
    Originally published : London : W. Collins Sons & Co., [c1923]
    1. Dogs—Anecdotes. I. Title. II. Scheffauer, Herman George
QL795.D6 M3   2002
636.7—dc21   2002066236

CONTENTS

FOREWORD

It was during the war that Thomas Mann, one of the great modern stylists, wrote this simple little idyll as a refuge and relief. It was a flight from the hideous realities of the world to the deeper realities of Nature, from the hate and inhumanity of man to the devotion and lovableness of the brute. This delectable symphony of human and canine psychology, of love of nature and of pensive humour, struck the true note of universality, a document packed with greater potencies in this direction than the deliberate, idealistic manifestos of the pacifists. It is for these reasons that the book has acquired a permanent charm, value, and significance, not only beyond the confines of the war and the confines of the author's own land and language, but also beyond those of the period.

In every land there still exists the same friendly and primitive relation between man and the dog, brought to its fullest expression of strength and beauty in the environment of the green world, rural or suburban.

Simple and unpretentious as a statement by Francis d'Assisi, yet full of a gentle modern sophistication and humour, this little work will bring delight and refreshment to all who seek flight from the heavy-laden hour. It is, moreover, one of the most subtle and penetrating studies of the psychology of the dog that has ever been written —tender yet unsentimental, realistic and full of the detail of masterly observation and description, yet in its final form and precipitation a work of exquisite literary art.

H. G. S.

BASHAN PUTS IN
HIS APPEARANCE

CHAPTER I

WHEN spring, which all men agree is the fairest season of the year, comes round again and happens to do honour to its name, I love to go for half an hour's stroll in the open air before breakfast. I take this stroll whenever the early chorus of the birds has succeeded in rousing me betimes—because I had been wise enough to terminate the preceding day at a seemly hour. And then I go walking—hatless—in the spacious avenue in front of my house, and sometimes in the parks which are more distant. Before I capitulate to the day's work, I long to draw a few draughts of young morning air and to taste the joy of the pure early freshness of things. Standing on the steps which lead down from my front door, I give a whistle. This whistle consists of two tones, a base tone and a deeper quarter-tone—as though I were beginning the first notes of the second phrase of Schubert's unfinished symphony, a signal which may be regarded as equal in tonal value to a name of two syllables.

The very next moment, as I go on towards the garden gate, a sound is heard in the distance, a sound at first almost inaudible, then growing rapidly nearer and clearer—a sound such as might ensue if a metal tag were to be set clinking against the brass trimmings of a leather collar. Then, as I turn round, I see Bashan curving in swift career around the corner of the house and heading for me full tilt as though he intended to knock me over. His efforts cause him to shorten his underlip a bit, so that two or three of his lower front teeth are laid bare. How splendidly they gleam in the early sun !

Bashan comes straight from his kennel.

This is situated behind the house under the floor of the veranda, which is supported on pillars. It is probable that, after a night of divers and unknown adventures, he had been enjoying a short morning doze in this kennel, until my two-syllabic whistle roused him to swift activity. This kennel or miniature hut is equipped with curtains made of coarse material, and is lined with straw. Thus it chances that a stray straw or two may be clinging to Bashan's coat—already rather ruffled up from his lying and stretching—or that one of these refractory straws may even be left sticking between his toes. This is a vision which always reminds me of the old Count Moor in Schiller's *Robbers*—as I once saw him in a most vivid and imaginative production, coming out of the Hunger Tower, with a straw between two of his toes.

Involuntarily I take up a flank position to the charging Bashan as he comes storming onward—an attitude of defence—for his apparent intention of lunging himself between my feet and laying me low is most amazingly deceptive. But always at the last moment and just before the collision, he manages to put on the brakes and to bring himself to—something which testifies to his physical as well as his mental self-control. And now —without uttering a sound—for Bashan makes but scant use of his sonorous and expressive voice—he begins to carry out a confused dance of welcome and salutation all about me, a dance consisting of rapid tramplings, of prodigious waggings—waggings which are not limited to that member which is intended for their proper expression —but which demand tribute of his entire hindquarters up to his very ribs, further-more an annular contraction of his body, as well as darting, far-flung leaps into the air, also rotations about his own axis—perform-ances which, strange to say, he endeavours to hide from my gaze, for whenever I turn towards him, he transfers them to the other side. The very moment, however, I bend down and stretch out my hand, he is brought suddenly with a single leap to my side. There he stands, like a statue, with his shoulder-blade pressing against my shin-bone. He stands aslant, with his strong paws braced against the ground, his face uplifted towards mine, so that he peers into my eyes from below and in a reversed direction. His stillness whilst I pat his shoulder and mutter friendly words, breathes forth the same concentration and emotion as the preceding delirium.

He is a short-haired setter—if you will not take this designation too sternly and strictly, but with a grain of salt. For Bashan cannot really claim to be a setter such as are described in books—a setter in accordance with the most meticulous laws and decrees. He is perhaps a trifle too small for this—for he is somewhat under the size of a full-fledged setter. And then his legs are not quite straight, but somewhat disposed to bend outward, a condition of things which would also be scarcely in accordance with the ideal of a Simon-pure breed.

The slight disposition to dewlaps or "wattles," that is, to those folds of skin about the neck which are capable of lending a dog such a dignified expression, becomes him admirably, though it is certain that this feature would also be objected to as a flaw by implacable experts on breeding, for I am told that in this species of dog the skin should lie close and firm about the throat.

Bashan's colouring is very beautiful. His coat is a rusty brown in the ground colour, striped with black. But there are also considerable mixtures of white. These predominate on the chest, the paws, and the belly. His entire nose, which is very short, seems to be painted black. This black and rusty brown makes a pretty velvety pattern on his broad skull as well as on his cool ear-laps. One of his most edifying external features is the whorl, tuft or tassel into which the white hair on his chest twists itself and which sticks out like the spike on certain ancient armour. To be sure, one of his rather arbitrary glories—the colour of his hair—might also appear a dubious point to those who rate racial laws higher than the values of personality. It is possible that the classic setter should be monochrome or decorated with shaded or toned spots, and not, like Bashan, with tiger-like stripes. But the most emphatic warning against classifying Bashan in any rigid or iron-clad category, is a certain drooping manner of the hirsute appendages about the corners of his mouth and the underside of his jaws, features which might not incorrectly be designated as a kind of bristling moustache and goatee—features which, if you will rivet your eye upon them from near or far, will remind you of a *griffon* or an Airedale terrier !

But what odds ?—setter or pointer or terrier—Bashan is a fine and handsome animal. Look at him as he leans rigidly against my knee and looks up at me with a profound and concentrated devotion ! His eye, ah, his eye ! is beautiful, soft, and wise, even though a trifle glassy and protuberant. The iris is a rusty brown—of the same colour as his coat, though it forms only a small ring in consequence of the tremendous expanse of the black mirrors of the pupils. On the outer periphery the colour blends into the white of the eye, swimming in it, as it were. The expression of his face, an expression of reasonable cheerfulness, proclaims the fine masculinity of his moral nature, which is reflected physically in the structure of his body. The vaulted chest, beneath whose smooth, supple, and clinging skin the ribs show powerfully, the drawn-in haunches, the nervous, clear-veined legs, the strong and well-shaped paws—all proclaim a brave heart and much virile virtue

—proclaim peasant blood—hunting blood. Yes, there can be no doubt of it—the hunter and the tracker dominate prodigiously in Bashan's education. He is a bona-fide setter —if you must know—even though he may not owe his existence to some snobbish bit of blue-blooded inbreeding. And this perhaps is what I would imply by the rather confused and unrelated words which I address to him whilst patting him on the shoulder-blade.

He stands and stares, listening intently to the tone of my voice. He finds that this tone is full of accents which decidedly approve of his existence, something which I am at pains to emphasise in my speech. And suddenly, with an upward lunge of the head and a swift opening and shutting of his jaws, he makes a snap towards my face, as though he intended to bite off my nose, a bit of pantomime that is obviously meant to be an answer to my remarks and which invariably throws me backward in a sudden recoil, laughing—as Bashan well knows. He intends this to be a kind of air-kiss, half tenderness, half mischievousness —a manœuvre which has been peculiar to him from puppyhood on—I had never observed it in the case of any of his prede- cessors. Moreover, he at once begs pardon for the liberty he has taken by waggings, short abrupt bows and an embarrassed air. And then we pass out of the garden-gate into the open.

We are now invested with a sound of rushing and roaring as of the sea. For my house fronts almost directly on the River Isar " rolling rapidly " as in the famous lines by Campbell, and foaming over flat terraces in its bed. We are separated from it only by the rows of poplars, by a strip of fenced-in grass which is planted with young maples and an elevated road which is fringed by great aspens, giants which conduct themselves in the same bizarre manner as willows and snow up the whole region with their white, seed-bearing fluff at the beginning of June. Up river, towards the city, I see a detachment of pioneers practising the building of a pontoon bridge. The thudding of their heavy boots upon the boards and the shouts of their officers echo across the stream. From the farther bank there come sounds of industrial activity, for yonder, at some distance down-stream from the house, there is a locomotive plant working under increased pressure—in accordance with the times. The tall windows of this great brick shed glow through the darkness at all hours of the night. New and beautifully lacquered engines hurry to and fro on their trial trips, a steam siren occasionally lets its heady howl be heard, a dull, thunderous pother makes the air quiver from time to time, and from the throats of several stacks the smoke creams darkly forth. This, however, is driven away by a kindly-disposed wind towards the distant tracts of woods, so that it seldom rolls across the river. Thus in the suburban, semi-rural solitude of this region, the whisperings of contemplative nature mingle with those of human activity. Over all lies the blank-eyed freshness of the morning hour.

According to the daylight-saving law, the time might be half-past seven when I take my walk; in reality it is half-past six. With arms crossed behind my back I stroll through the tender sunshine down the poplar-lined avenue, barred by the long shadows of the trees. From here I cannot see the river, but its broad and even flow is audible. There is a soft whispering in the trees, the penetrating twittering, fluting, chirping, and sob-like trill of the songbirds fills the air. Under the moist blue heavens an aeroplane coming from the east, a stark mechanical bird with a roaring voice, now swelling, and now softly ebbing away, steers its independent way across land and river, and Bashan delights my eye with beautiful

leaps at full length to and fro across the low
fence of the grass plot to the left.

Bashan is jumping because he actually
knows that I take pleasure in his jumping.
Often by means of calls and knockings
upon the fence, have I encouraged him in
it and praised him when he had fulfilled my
wishes.   And now, too, he comes after
almost every jump so that I may tell him
that he is a daring and elegant fence-vaulter,
at which he also ventures a jump or two
towards my face and beslobbers my thrust-
out, defensive arm with the slaver of his
mouth.   These exercises, however, he likewise intends to be a kind of gymnastic
morning toilet, for he smooths his ruffled
coat by means of these athletic movements
and rids himself of the straws which had
disfigured it.

It is good thus to go walking in the
morning, the senses rejuvenated, the spirit
purged by the healing bath and long Lethean
draught of the night.   You look upon the

day that lies before you, regard it with strong, serene confidence, but you hesitate lazily to begin it—you are master of an unusually free and unburdened span of time lying between the dream and the day, your reward for the good use you have made of your time. The illusion that you are leading a life that is constant, simple, undissipated and benignly introspective, the illusion that you belong utterly to yourself, renders you happy. Man is disposed to regard his case or condition of the moment, be this glad or troubled, peaceful or passionate, for the true, essential, and permanent aspect of his life, and above all is in fancy inclined to elevate every happy *ex tempore* to a radiant rule and an unbreakable habit, whereas he is really condemned to live by improvisation, from hand to mouth, so to speak.

So, drawing in deep breaths of the morning air, you believe in your freedom and in your worth, though you ought to be aware, and at heart *are* aware, that the world is

holding its snares ready to entangle you in
them, and that in all probability you will
again be lying in bed until nine to-morrow
morning, because you had got into it at
two the night before, heated, befogged, and
full of passionate debate. . . . Well, so be
it. To-day you are the man of sobriety and
the dew-clad early hour, the right royal
lord of that mad hunter yonder who is
just making another jump across the fence
out of sheer joy that you are apparently
content to live this day with him and not
waste it upon the world you have left behind
you.

We follow the tree-lined avenue for about
five minutes, to that point where it ceases
to be a road and becomes a coarse desert of
gravel parallel to the course of the river.
We turn our backs upon this and strike
into a broad, finely-gravelled street which,
like the poplar-lined road, is equipped with
a cycle-path, but is still void of houses.
This leads to the right, between low-lying

allotments of wooded land, towards the declivity which bounds our river-banks —Bashan's field of action towards the east.

We cross another street of an equally futuristic nature, which runs openly between the woods and the meadows, and which, farther up in the direction of the city and the tram-stop, is lined with a compact mass of flats. A slanting pebble path leads us to a prettily arranged dingle, almost like a *kurgarten* to the eye, but void of all humanity, like the entire district at this hour. There are benches along the rounded walks—which enlarge themselves here and there to *rondels* or to trim playgrounds for the children and to spacious planes of grass on which are growing old and well-formed trees with deep pendant crowns, revealing only a short stretch of trunk above the grass. There are elms, beeches, limes, and silvery willows in parklike groups. I find great pleasure in this carefully-groomed park, in which I could not wander more undisturbed, if it were my own. It is perfect and complete. The gravel paths which curve down and around the gentle, sloping lawns, are even equipped with stone gutters. And there are far and pleasing glimpses between all this greenery, the architecture of a few villas which peer in from both sides and form the background.

Here for a little while, I stroll to and fro upon the walks, whilst Bashan, his body inclined in a centrifugal plane, and drunk with joy of the fetterless unlimited space about him, executes gallopades criss and cross and head over heels upon the smooth grassy surfaces. Or else with barkings wherein indignation and pleasure mix and mingle, he pursues some bird, which, either bewitched by fear or out of sheer mischief, flutters along always a few inches in front of his open jaws. But no sooner do I sit down upon a bench than he comes and takes up a position on my foot. It is one of the immutable laws of his life that he will run about only when I myself am in motion, and that as soon as I sit down he too should become inactive. The necessity for this is not quite obvious, but to Bashan it is as the laws of the Medes and Persians.

It is quaint, cosy, and amusing to feel him sitting upon my foot and penetrating it with the feverish glow of his body. A sense of gaiety and sympathy fills my bosom, as always when I am abandoned to him and to his idea of things. His manner of sitting is a bit peasant-like, a bit uncouth—with his shoulder-blades turned outward and his paws turned in, irregularly. In this position his figure appears smaller and stockier than it really is, and the white whorl of hair upon his chest is thrust into comic prominence. But his head is thrown back in the most dignified manner and redeems his disregard for a fine pose by virtue of the intense concentrated attention it displays.

It is so quiet that both of us remain absolutely still. The rushing of the water reaches us only in a subdued murmur. Under such conditions the tiny secret activities in our immediate world take on a particular importance and preoccupy the senses,—the brief rustling of a lizard, the note of a bird, the burrowing of a mole in the ground. Bashan's ears are erected, in so far as the muscular structure of flapping ears admits of this. He cocks his head in order to intensify his sense of hearing. And the nostrils of his moist black nose are in incessant and sensitive motion, responsive to innumerable subtle reactions.

He then lies down once more, being careful, however, to maintain his contact with my foot. He is lying in a profile position, in the ancient, well-proportioned, animalistic, idol-like attitude of the sphinx, with elevated head and breast, his thighs pressed close to his body, his paws extended in front of him. He is overheated, so he opens his jaws, a manœuvre which causes the concentrated cleverness of his expression to pass into the purely bestial. His eyes twinkle and narrow to mere slits, and between his white and strong triangular teeth a long, rose-red tongue lolls forth.

HOW WE ACQUIRED BASHAN

CHAPTER II

HOW WE ACQUIRED BASHAN

IT was a short, buxom, dark-eyed young woman who, with the help of her equally sturdy and dark-eyed daughter, keeps a hillside tavern not far from the Bavarian mountain resort called Tolz, who acted as go-between in the business of our making Bashan's acquaintance and then acquiring him. That is over two years ago and he was only half a year old at the time. Anastasia —this is the name of mine hostess—knew that we had been compelled to have our Percy shot—he was a Scotch collie, a harmless, somewhat weak-minded aristocrat, who had been visited in his old age by a painful and disfiguring skin disease—and that for over a year we had been without a faithful guardian. She therefore rang us up from her perch in the hills and told us that she was boarding a dog who was sure to suit us to a dot, and that he was to be seen at any time.

The children coaxed and urged, and as the curiosity of their elders was scarcely less than their own, we all sallied forth the very next afternoon to climb the heights where Anastasia's tavern lay. We found her in her roomy kitchen which was filled with warm and succulent vapours. There she stood with her round bare forearms and her dress open at the throat, with her face rosy and shiny, preparing the evening meal for her boarders, whilst her daughter, busily but quietly going to and fro, lent assistance. We were given a pleasant greeting, and the fact that we had not postponed our visit but had come to attend to business without delay, was favourably commented upon. In answer to our inquisitive glances, Resi, the daughter, steered us toward the kitchen table. Here she bent down, placed her

hands upon her knees, and directed a few
flattering and encouraging words under the
table. There, tied to a table-leg with a
frazzled rope, stood a creature of whom we
had until then been unaware in the smouldering half-light of this kitchen. It was a
vision, however, which would have induced
any one to burst into peals of pitying
laughter.

There he stood on long, knock-kneed
legs, his tail between them, his four feet
close together, his back arched. He was
trembling. It is possible that he was trembling out of fear, but one had the impression
that it was due to a lack of flesh and fat.
For the little apparition before us was a
mere skeleton, a chest with a spinal column
covered with rough hair and supported on
four sticks. He had drawn back his ears,
a muscular manœuvre which, of course,
immediately extinguishes every gleam of
intelligent cheerfulness in a dog's physiog-
nomy. This effect in his still so childish

face was so extreme that it expressed nothing but stupidity and misery as well as an insistent plea for consideration. There was also the fact to consider that the appendage which one might now call his goatee was at that time still more developed in relation to the rest of his face, something which gave to the aggregate woebegoneness of his appearance a trace of sour hypochondria.

We all bent down to address comforting and coaxing words to this picture of misery. Anastasia, from her post in front of the stove, mingled her remarks with the rapturous and pitying exclamations of the children, and retailed information as to the personality of her boarder. His name, she declared in her pleasant and even voice, was, for the time being, Lux. He was the son of most respectable parents. She was personally acquainted with his mother, and as for his father she had heard nothing but good of him. Lux was born on a farm at Huglfing, and it was only owing to special circumstances that his owners were willing to sell him so cheaply. For that reason they had brought him to the tavern—in view of the lively traffic there. They had come in a small wagon and Lux had gallantly trotted the whole twenty kilometres, between the hind wheels. She had at once thought of us, for she knew we were looking for a good dog, and she felt quite certain that we could not help taking him. If we could decide upon taking him at once, it would be a fine thing all round. She was sure that we would have great joy of him, and as for him, he would no longer be alone in the world, but have a cosy berth, and she, Anastasia, would cease to worry about him. We ought, however, not to be prejudiced against him because of the faces he was now making. He was a bit cowed at present and not sure of himself, because of the strange surroundings. But we

would soon see that he had a fine
pedigree, that his parents were excellent
stock.

Yes, we objected, but it was clear—was it
not—that these parents of his had not been
well matched ?

Oh, yes, they had, and both of them were
a fine breed, too ! She, Anastasia, would
guarantee that his points were all good. He
was also unspoiled and very moderate in
his demands—something which was worth
a good deal in such lean times as these. Up
to the present he had supported himself
entirely on potato-skins. She suggested
that we take him home first, on probation,
as it were. We were under no obligation
at all. In case we did not like him she
would take him back and return the small
sum we had paid. She was not afraid to
say this—not afraid that we might take her
at her word. For knowing us as she did, and
knowing *him*, too—both parties to the bargain
—she was convinced that we should learn

to love him and never think of ever giving
him up again.

She said a good deal more in this vein—
quietly, glowingly, and amiably—the while
she negotiated things on the stove, with the
flames at times shooting up magically in
front of her. And finally she came herself
and with both hands opened Lux's mouth
in order to show us his fine teeth and for
some mysterious reason also the rosy and
riffled roof of his mouth.

Upon our asking, with professional air,
whether he had already had the mange, she
replied with a slight show of impatience,
that she did not know. And as to his size
when he had finally stopped growing ?—
well, she declared with a smart promptness,
this would be exactly that of our deceased
Percy. There was a good deal more of
talk to and fro, a good deal of warm-hearted
encouragement on the part of Anastasia,
reinforced by pleas from the children, and
a good deal of half-conquered irresolution

on our part. We finally begged leave to be permitted to consider the matter for a short time, and this was graciously granted us. And so we descended to the valley, thoughtfully rehearsing and ruminating upon our impressions.

That bit of four-legged misery under the table had naturally captured the hearts of the children, and we grown-ups attempted in vain to smile away their lack of taste and judgment. We, too, felt a tugging at our hearts and realised all too clearly that we should be hard put to it to banish the vision of the unfortunate Lux from our memories. What was to become of him? —if we turned away in contumely? Into whose—into what hands would he fall? A terrible and mysterious figure arose in our phantasies: the knacker in his flaying-house, from whose loathsome attentions we had once saved Percy by means of a few chivalrous bullets from the rifle of a game-keeper and the honourable burial-place we

had given him at the edge of our garden.
If we were minded to leave Lux to an unknown and possibly ghastly fate we should
not have been so careless as to make his
acquaintance, and to look upon his childish
face with the goatee. But now that we were
aware of his existence, a responsibility seemed
laid upon us which we could dispute only
with difficulty and with forced, half-hearted
denials.

Thus it came about that the third day
following saw us once more climbing up
that gentle spur of the lower Alps. It was
not that we had already decided upon the
acquisition of Lux. But we saw that
things being as they were, it was not
likely that the matter would have any other
outcome.

This time we found Anastasia and her
daughter sitting opposite each other at the
kitchen-table and drinking coffee. Between
them, in front of the table, sat he who bore
the preliminary name of Lux—sat as he is

still accustomed to sit to-day, his shoulder-
blades twisted like a yokel's, his paws turned
in. Under his worn leather collar there
was a little nosegay of wild-flowers which
decidedly augmented his appearance and
lent it something festive, like that of an
enterprising village youth on a Sunday or
the bridegroom at a country wedding. The
young hostess, who herself made a neat
and pretty appearance in her peasant costume
with its laced velvet bodice, had furbished
him out in this fashion in order to celebrate
his entry into his new home—as she put it.
And mother and daughter both assured us
that they had been absolutely certain that
we should come again to fetch Lux, and
that they knew that we should come to-
day.

Thus all further controversy and debate
proved to be impossible, in fact, precluded
almost before we had entered. In her own
pleasant way, Anastasia thanked us for the
purchase-money which we handed to her

and which amounted to ten marks. It was
clear that she had imposed this price upon
us more in our own interests than in hers,
or those of the farmer-folk who had Lux
to sell—that is, she felt that it was necessary
to give a positive, computable value to poor
Lux in our eyes. This we understood and
gladly paid the tribute. Lux was detached
from his table-leg, the end of the rope
handed over to me, and thus we passed over
the threshold of Anastasia's kitchen, our
procession attended by the most friendly
wishes and congratulations.

It was, however, not a triumphal procession which proceeded on the hour's march
towards home with our new household companion—the less so since our bridegroom
soon lost his nosegay. It is true that we read
amusement and also mocking and derogatory
depreciation in the glances of the people we
met, the opportunities for which became
multiplied as we made our way through
the market place—longitudinally. To cap

everything we soon discovered that Lux was suffering from a disorder of the bowels, apparently a chronic one, something which forced us to make frequent halts under the cynical eyes of the townspeople. We formed a protective circle and hid his internal misery from rude eyes, and solemnly asked ourselves whether it was not, after all, the mange which was thus displaying its most sinister symptoms? But this anxiety was uncalled-for, as the future proved to us, for we soon saw that we had to deal with a sound and hearty constitution which has proved itself proof against plagues and distempers up to this very moment.

As soon as we reached home, the servant-maids were called forth, so that they might make acquaintance with this new addition to the family and also deliver their humble judgment upon him. We saw that they had been prepared to express admiration, but after they had caught sight of him and read our own vacillating and uncertain looks, they broke into rude laughter, turned their backs upon him of the rueful countenance, and made motions of rejection in his direction. Confirmed by this in our doubt as to whether they would fully appreciate the humanitarian nature of the small fee which Anastasia had demanded, we declared that the dog had been presented to us. And then we led Lux to the veranda and set before him a welcoming feast composed of liberal scraps of considerable content.

But his timidity caused him to reject all this. He sniffed, to be sure, at the titbits which he was invited to consume, but stood aside shy and incapable of bringing himself to the pitch of believing that all these cheese-rinds and chicken-bones were really intended for him. On the other hand, he did not reject the sack which we had stuffed with seaweed and which we had made ready upon the floor for his comfort. And there he lay down with his paws tucked under him, whilst we retired to the inner rooms and consulted as to the name which he was finally to bear through all the years to come.

He still refused to eat on the following day. Then followed a period during which he devoured indiscriminately everything that came within the radius of his jaws, until he attained the necessary degree of quiet regularity and critical dignity in matters of diet. The process of his domiciling and civic habitation should be described in some bold and spacious manner. I shall not lose myself in a too meticulous portrayal of this process. It suffered an interruption through the temporary disappearance of Bashan. The children had led him into the garden and they had taken off the rope in order to give him freedom of action. During an unguarded moment he had escaped into the vastness of the outer world through the gap left between the lower part of the gate and the gravel path. His disappearance aroused grief and consternation—at least

among the master and mistresses of the
house, for the servants were disposed to
make light of the loss of a gift-dog, if they
really regarded it as a loss at all.

The telephone began to play tempes-
tuously between our domain and Anastasia's
mountain caravanserai, at which we hope-
fully adjudged him to be. But in vain,
he had not shown himself there. Two days
heavy with care went by, and then Anastasia
reported that she had received tidings from
Huglfing that Lux had appeared at the
parental farm an hour and a half ago. He
was there, no denying it—the idealism of
his instinct had drawn him back to the world
of potato-parings. And in lonely one-day
marches, facing all kinds of wind and
weather, he had covered the twenty kilometres which he had once travelled between
the wheels of the farm wagon. And so
his former owners were obliged to hitch
up this vehicle in order to deliver the
fugitive home-comer into Anastasia's hands

once more. Two more days rolled by and then we again went forth to bring home the errant one. We found him fastened as before to the table-leg, unkempt and gaunt and splashed with the mud of the country roads. To be sure, he gave signs of recognition and of joy as he caught sight of us. But why then had he left us?

There came a time when it was clear that he had rid his mind of the charms of the farm, but had not yet fully taken root with us, so that his soul was masterless and like to a leaf that is set tumbling about by the wind. During this period it was necessary to keep a sharp eye on him whilst out walking, for he was all too prone to tear asunder unperceived the weak band of sympathy that bound us, and in a grand burst of independent living to lose himself in the woods—where he would certainly have reverted to the condition of his savage forbears. Our solicitude preserved him from this sinister destiny. We strove to keep him on that high moral level which his kind had achieved at the side of man during thousands of years of association in common. And then a radical change of residence—our removal to the city, or rather its suburbs— led to his becoming wholly dependent upon us and entering upon an intimate connection with our household life.

REGARDING BASHAN'S CHARACTER

CHAPTER III

A FEW ITEMS REGARDING BASHAN'S CHARACTER AND MANNER OF LIFE

A MAN in the Valley of the Isar had told me that dogs of this species might become obnoxious, for they were always anxious to be with the master. I was therefore warned against accepting the tenacious faithfulness which Bashan soon began to display towards me as all too personal in its origin. On the other hand, this made it easier for me to discourage it a little—in so far as this may, in self-defence, have been necessary. We have to deal here with a remote and long-derived patriarchal instinct of the dog which determines him—at least so far as the more manly, open-air loving breeds are concerned—to regard and honour the man, the head of the house and the family, as the master, the protector of the home, the lord, and to find the goal and meaning of his existence in a peculiar relationship of loyal vassal-friendship, and in the maintenance of a far greater spirit of independence towards the other members of the family. It was this spirit that Bashan manifested towards me from the very beginning. His eyes followed me about with a manly trustfulness shining in them. He seemed to be asking for commands which he might fulfil but which I chose not to give, since obedience was not one of his strong points. He clung to my heels with the visible conviction that his inseparability from me was something firmly rooted in the sacred nature of things.

It went without saying that in the family circle he would lie down only at *my* feet and never at any one else's. It went equally without saying that in case I should separate from the others when out walking and pursue my own ways, he should join me and follow *my* footsteps. He also insisted upon my company when I was working, and when he chanced to find the door that gave upon the garden closed, he would come vaulting in through the window with startling suddenness, whereby a good deal of gravel would come rattling in upon the floor, and then with a sob and a sigh he would throw himself under my desk.

But there is a reverence which we pay to life and to living things which is too vigilant and keen not to be violated even by a dog's presence when we feel the need of being alone, and it was then that Bashan always disturbed me in the most tangible fashion. He would step up to my chair, wag his tail, look at me with devouring glances, and keep up an incessant trampling. The slightest receptive or approving movement on my part would result in his climbing up on the arm-rests of the chair, and glueing himself against my chest, in order to force me to laugh by the air-kisses which he kept lunging in my direction. And then he would proceed to an investigation of the top of my desk, assuming, no doubt, that something edible was to be found there, since I was so often caught bending over it. And then his broad and hairy paws would smear or blur the wet ink of my manuscript.

Called sharply to account, he would lie down once more and fall asleep. But no sooner was he asleep than he would begin to dream, during which he would execute the movements of running with all his four feet stretched out, at the same time giving vent to a clear yet subdued ventriloquistic barking which sounded as if it came from another world. That this had a disturbing and distracting effect upon me need surprise no one, for, first of all, it was eerie, and then it stirred and burdened my conscience. This dream-life was all too clearly an artificial substitute for the real chase, the real hunt, and was prepared for him by his nature, because in his common life with me, the happiness of unrestrained movement in the open did not devolve upon him in that measure which his blood and his instincts demanded. This came home to me very strongly, but as it was not to be altered, it was necessary that my moral disquietude should be dispelled by an appeal to other and higher interests. This led me to affirm that he brought a great deal of mud into the room during bad weather, and moreover, that he tore the carpets with his claws. Hence, as a matter of principle, he was forbidden to remain in the house or to bear me company as long as I chanced to be in the house—even though occasional exceptions were made. He understood this law at once and submitted to the unnatural prohibition, since it was precisely this which expressed in itself the inscrutable will of the master and lord of the house.

For this remoteness from me, which often continues, especially in the winter, for the greater part of the day, is merely a matter of being away—no actual separation or lack of connection. He is no longer with me—by my orders—but then that is merely the carrying-out of an order, after all a kind of negative being-with-me, as he would say. As for any independent life which Bashan might lead without me during these hours—that is not to be thought of. Through the glass door of my study I see him disporting in a clumsy, uncle-like manner with the children on the small patch of grass in front of the house. But constantly he comes running up to the door, and as he cannot see me through the muslin curtain which stretches across the pane, he sniffs at the crack between door and jamb so as to assure himself of my presence, and then sits down on the steps with his back turned towards the room, mounting guard. From my writing-table I can also see him moving at a thoughtful trot between the old aspens on the elevated highway yonder. But such promenades are merely a tepid pastime

devoid of pride, joy, and life. And it
would be unutterably unthinkable that
Bashan should take to devoting himself to
the glorious pleasures of the chase upon his
own account, even though no one would
hinder him from doing this, and my presence,
as will be shown later, would not be particularly favourable towards such an objec-
tive.

He begins to live only when I go forth—
though, alas, he cannot always be said to
begin life even then ! For after I leave the
house the question is whether I am going
to turn towards the right, that is, down the
avenue that leads into the open and to the
solitude of our hunting-grounds, or towards
the left in the direction of the tram station
in order to ride to the city and into the great
and spacious world. It is only in the first
instance that Bashan finds that there is any
sense in accompanying me. At first he joined
me after I had chosen the great and spacious
world, regarded with vast astonishment

the car as it came thundering on, and,
forcibly suppressing his shyness, made a
blind and loyal jump upon the platform,
directly amongst the passengers. But the
storm of public indignation swept him off
again, and so he resolved to go galloping
alongside the roaring vehicle—which bore
so little resemblance to the farm wagon
between the wheels of which he had once
trotted. Faithfully he kept step as long as
this was possible, and his wind would no
doubt have held out too. But being a son
of the upland farm, he was lost in the traffic
of the metropolis; he got between people's
legs, strange dogs made flank attacks upon
him; a tumult of wild odours such as he
had never before experienced, vexed and
confused his senses; house-corners, impreg-
nated with the essences of old adventures,
lured him irresistibly. He remained behind,
and though he once more overtook the wagon
on rails, this proved to be a wrong one,
even though it exactly resembled the right

one.   Bashan ran blindly in the wrong
direction, lost himself more and more in
the disconcerting strangeness of the world.
And it was more than two days before he
came home, starved and limping—to that
last house along the river to which his
master had also been sensible enough to
return in the meantime.

This happened two or three times, then
Bashan finally gave up accompanying me
when I turned towards the left.   He knows
instantly what I intend to do as soon as I
emerge from the doorway of the house—
make a trip to the hunting-grounds or a
trip to the great world.   He jumps up from
the door-mat upon which he has been awaiting my coming forth under the protecting
arch of the entrance.   He jumps up and at
the same moment he sees what my intentions
are.   My clothing betrays these to him, the
cane that I carry, also my attitude and
expression, the cool and preoccupied look I
give him, or the irritation and challenge in

my eyes. He understands. Headlong he plunges down the steps and goes dancing before me in swift and sudden bounds and full of excitement towards the gate when my going forth seems to be certain. But when he beholds hope vanish, he subsides within himself, lays his ears close to his head and his eyes take on that expression of shy misery which is found in contrite sinners—that look which misfortune begets in the eyes of men and also of animals.

At times he is really unable to believe what he sees and knows, that it is all up and that there is no use hoping for a hunt. His desires have been too intense. He repudiates the signs and symbols—chooses not to see the city walking-stick, the careful citified clothes I am wearing. He pushes through the gate with me, switches around outside in a half turn, and seeks to draw me towards the right by starting to gallop in this direction and by turning his head towards me, forces himself to overlook the

fateful No which I oppose to his efforts.
He comes back when I actually do turn
towards the left, accompanies me, snorting
deeply, and ejaculating short, confused high
notes which seem to arise from the tremendous tension in his interior, as I walk
along the fence of the garden, and then he
begins to jump back and forth over the
pickets of the adjacent public park. These
pickets are rather high, and he groans a
little in his flight through the air out of
fear lest he hurt himself. He makes these
leaps impelled by a kind of desperate gaiety,
scornful of all hard facts, and also to bribe
me, to work upon my sympathies by his
cleverness. For it is not yet quite *impossible*
—however improbable it may seem—that I
may nevertheless leave the city path at the
end of the park, once more turn towards
the left and lead him on to liberty—even if
only by way of the slightly roundabout
way to the post-box. This happens, it is
true, but it happens only rarely. Once this

hope has dissolved into empty air, Bashan
settles down upon his haunches and lets
me go my way.

There he sits now, in yokel-like, ungrace-
ful attitude, in the very middle of the road,
and stares after my retreating form, down
the whole long vista. If I turn my head,
he pricks up his ears, but does not follow
me. Nor would he follow me if I should
call or whistle—he knows this would all
be to no purpose. Even from the very end
of the avenue I can see him still sitting
there, a small, dark, awkward shape in the
middle of the highroad. A pang goes
through my heart—I mount the tram with
an uneasy conscience. He has waited so
long and so patiently—and who does not know
what torture waiting can be ! His whole
life is nothing but waiting—for the next
walk in the open—and this waiting begins
as soon as he has rested after his last run.
During the night, too, he waits, for his

slumbers are distributed throughout the entire twenty-four hours of the sun's revolution, and many a siesta upon the smooth lawn, whilst the sun beats upon his coat, or behind the curtains of his hut, must help to shorten the bare and empty spaces of the day. His nocturnal rest is therefore dismembered and without unity. He is driven by blind impulses hither and thither in the darkness, through the yard and the garden—he runs from place to place—and waits. He waits for the recurrent visit of the local watchman with the lantern, the heavy thud of whose footfall he accompanies against his own better knowledge with a terrible burst of heralding barks. He waits for the paling of the heavens, the crowing of the cock in the near-by nursery-garden, the stir of the morning wind in the trees, and for the unlocking of the kitchen entrance, so that he may slip in and warm himself at the white-tiled range.

But I believe that the torture of this

nightly vigil is mild, compared to that which
Bashan must endure in the broad of day,
particularly when the weather is fair, be it
winter or summer, when the sun lures into
the open, and the desire for violent motion
tugs in every muscle, and his master, without
whom, of course, there can be no real enjoy-
ment, persistently refuses to leave his seat
behind the glass door.

Bashan's mobile little body, through which
life pulsates so swiftly and feverishly, has
been, so to speak, exhausted with rest—
and there can be no thought of sleep. Up
he comes to the terrace in front of my door,
drops himself in the gravel with a sob
which comes from the very depths of his
being, and lays his head upon his paws,
turning up his eyes with a martyr's expression towards heaven. This, however, lasts
only a few seconds, the new position irks
him at once, he feels it to be untenable.
There is still one thing he can do. He may
descend the steps and pay attention to a

small tree trimmed in the shape of a rose-tree and flanking the beds of roses, an unfortunate tree which, owing to these visits of Bashan, dwindles away every year and must be replanted. There he stands on three legs, melancholy and contemplative —the slave of a habit, whether urged by Nature or not. Then he reverts to his four legs, and is no better off than before. Dumbly he gazes aloft into the branches of a group of ash-trees. Two birds are flitting from bough to bough with lively twitterings—he watches the feathered ones dashing away swift as arrows, and turns aside, seeming to shrug his shoulders at so much childish *élan* of life.

He stretches and strains as though he intended to tear himself asunder. This undertaking, for the sake of thoroughness, he divides into two parts: first of all, he stretches his front legs, lifting his hindquarters into the air, and then exercises these by stretching his hind legs far behind him.

He yawns tremendously both times, with wide, red-gaping jaws and upcurled tongue. Well, now he has also achieved this—the performance cannot be carried on any further, and having once stretched yourself according to all the rules of the game, it is inconceivable that you should immediately repeat the manœuvre. So Bashan stands and gazes at the ground. Then he begins to turn himself slowly and searchingly about his own axis as though he wished to lie down and were not as yet certain as to the way in which this should be done. He changes his mind, however, and goes with lazy step to the middle of the lawn, where with a sudden, almost convulsive movement, he hurls himself upon his back in order to cool and scour this by a lively rolling hither and thither upon the mown surface of grass.

This must induce a mighty feeling of bliss, for stiffly he draws up his paws as he rolls and snaps into the air in all directions in a tumult of joy and satisfaction. All the more passionately he drains this rapture to the very dregs in that he knows that it is purely a fleeting rapture, and that one cannot very well wallow in this fashion more than ten seconds, and that that beneficent weariness which comes to one after such honest and happy efforts will not follow—but merely disillusion and two-fold disquietude—the price paid for this delirium, this drug-like dissipation. For a moment he lies with twisted eyeballs upon his side as though he were dead. Then he rises and shakes himself. He shakes himself as only his kind is able to shake itself—without having to fear a concussion of the brain. He shakes himself to a crescendo of flappings and rattlings, and his ears go slapping under his jawbone and his loose lips part from his white, bare triangular teeth.

And then ? Then he stands motionless, in stark abstraction. He has reached the ultimate limit and no longer has a single idea as to what he shall do with himself.

Under such circumstances as these, he has recourse to something extreme. He climbs up to the terrace, approaches the glass door —scratches only once and very feebly. But this soft and timidly lifted paw, this soft, solitary scratching, upon which he had resolved, after all other counsel had failed, work mightily upon me, and I arise to open the door for him in order to let him in, although I know that this can lead to no good. For he immediately begins to leap and cavort, as a call to engage in manly enterprises. He pushes the carpet into a hundred folds, spreads confusion through the room, and my peace and quiet are at an end.

But now judge whether it is easy for me to sail off in the tram, after seeing Bashan wait thus, and leave him sitting as a melancholy little heap of misery deep within the converging lines of the avenue of poplars !

When the summer is on and the daylight is long and lingering, this misfortune may

not be so overwhelming, for then there is
always a good chance that at least my evening
promenade will take me out into the open,
so that Bashan, even though the period of
waiting be arduous, may nevertheless still
meet with his reward and, provided one has
a certain amount of luck, be able to chase
a rabbit.   But in winter, it is all up for this
day and Bashan must bury all hope for a
full twenty-four hours.   For then the night
will have already fallen upon the hour of
my second going-forth ; the hunting grounds
are buried in impenetrable darkness, and I
must direct my steps towards regions arti-
ficially lighted, upstream, through streets
and public parks, and this does not suit
Bashan's nature and simplicity of soul.   It
is true that at first he followed me even
here, but soon gave this up and remained
at home.   It was not only that visible chances
for gadding about were lacking—the half-
dark made him hesitant, he shied in confused
alarm at man and bush.   The sudden

flapping of a policeman's cape caused him
to jump aside with a howl, and with the
courage of horror to make a sudden dash
at the policeman, who was also scared half
to death and strove to even up the fright he
had received by a torrent of harsh and
threatening words directed at me and Bashan.
And there were many other uncomfortable
encounters whenever he went forth with me
through the night and the mist. Apropos
of this policeman, I will remark that there
are three kinds of human beings to whom
Bashan has a whole-hearted aversion—namely
policemen, monks, and chimney-sweeps. He
cannot tolerate them, and will sally forth
against them with furious barks whenever
they go past the house, or wherever they
may chance to cross his path.

Moreover, winter is that season in which
the world lies most vigilantly and insolently
in ambush against our liberties and our
virtues, and least willingly grants us a
uniform and serene existence, an existence

of seclusion and of quiet preoccupation, and
so it happens that often the city draws me
to itself a second time in one day—in the
evening—when Society demands its rights.
Then, late, at midnight, the last tram de-
posits me far out at its penultimate stop.
Or I come jogging along on foot, long after
the last tram has returned to town—I come
wandering *distrait*, tempered with wine,
smoking, having passed the bourne of natural
fatigue and wrapped in a sense of false
security in relation to all things mundane.
And then it happens that the embodiment
of my own domesticity, as it were, my very
retirement, comes to meet me and salutes
and welcomes me not only without reproach
or touchiness, but with extreme joy, and
re-introduces me to my own fireside—all in
the shape of Bashan himself. It is pitch
dark, and the river goes by with a rushing
sound as I turn into the poplar avenue. A
few steps more and I feel that I am be-
capered and be-switched by paws and tail

—and have no clear idea of what is happening to me.

" Bashan ? " I ask of the darkness.

And then the capering and the switching are intensified to the utmost. They pass into something dervish- and Berserker-like, though the silence continues. The very moment I stand still I feel two homely and wet and muddy paws upon the lapels of my overcoat, and there are such violent snappings and lappings close to my face, that I bend backward, whilst I pat those lean shoulders, wet with rain or snow.

Yes, the dear fellow has waited for me at the tram-stop, well aware of my comings and goings and doings ; he had gone forth when the hour seemed to have arrived, and waited for me at the station—waited, perhaps, a long and weary while in the snow or rain. And his joy at my arrival is devoid of all resentment at my cruel faithlessness, even though I had utterly neglected him to-day and reduced all his hopes and expectances to naught. So I am loud in my praise of him as I pat his shoulders and we turn towards home. I tell him that he has acted nobly, and deliver myself of momentous promises with regard to the day which is already under way. I assure him (that is to say not so much him as myself) that we shall go hunting together to-morrow without fail, no matter what the weather. Amidst resolutions such as these, my mood of universality evaporates, seriousness and sobriety slink back into my soul, and my fancy, now full of the hunting-grounds and their loneliness, is seized by apperceptions of higher, secret and wondrous obligations.

But I am moved to add further details to this transcript of Bashan's character, so that the willing reader may see it in the *n*th degree of vivid verisimilitude. I might perhaps proceed with more or less skill by drawing a comparison between Bashan and the lamented Percy, for a contrariety more sharply defined than that which distinguished their respective natures is scarcely conceivable within one and the same species. As a basic consideration one must remember that Bashan enjoys perfect mental health, whilst Percy, as I have already intimated, was—as is not uncommon with dogs of blue-blooded pedigrees—a perfect fool his whole life long, crazy, a very model of overbred impossibility. Mention of this has been made in a more momentous connection, in a previous chapter.

I would merely mention here as a contrast Bashan's simple and popular ways as these manifest themselves when going for walks or when making salutations—occasions upon which the enunciation of his emotions remains within the bounds of common sense and a sound heartiness without ever touching the limits of hysteria—limits which Percy often transgressed on these occasions and that in the most disconcerting fashion.

But the whole antithesis between the two

creatures is by no means exhausted in this
—for this antithesis is in truth a mixed and
complicated one. Bashan, you must know,
is somewhat crude, like the common people
themselves, but, like them, also soft and
sentimental, whilst his noble predecessor
combined more delicacy and possibilities of
pain with an incomparably prouder and
firmer spirit, and despite his silliness, far
excelled that old yokel Bashan in the matter
of self-discipline. It is not in defence of an
aristocratic cult of values that I call attention to this mixture of opposite qualities,
of coarseness and tenderness, of delicacy
and resolution, but purely in the interests
of life and actuality. Bashan, for example,
is just the man for spending even the coldest
winter nights in the open, that is on the
straw behind the coarse burlap curtains of
his kennel. A slight affection of the bladder
prevents him from spending seven hours
uninterruptedly in a locked room without
committing a nuisance—a weakness of his

which caused us to lock him out during the inhospitable time of the year, setting a justifiable faith in his robust health. Only once, after a particularly icy and foggy night, did he make his appearance with moustaches and goatee miraculously frosted and iced and with that jerky, one-syllabic cough peculiar to dogs—but a few hours, and lo, he had conquered the cold and was none the worse for it.

But never would we have dared to expose the silken-haired Percy to the inclemency of such a night. On the other hand, Bashan stands in great fear of even the slightest pain, and every twinge wrings from him a response, the whining complaint of which would arouse aversion, if its naive, folkish quality did not disarm one and set the springs of gaiety aflow. Again and again, during his prowlings in the underwood, I have heard him squeal aloud—a thorn had chanced to prick him, or a resilient branch had switched him across the face, and if he happened to have scratched his belly a little in vaulting over the fence, or sprained his foot, I have been treated to an antique hero's chorus, a three-legged limping approach, an uncontrollable wailing and self-lamentation. And the more sympathetically I talked to him, the more insistent his clamour became—though in a quarter of an hour he would be swooping and running about as madly as before.

Percy was of a different metal. Percy would grit his teeth and keep mum. He feared the rawhide whip just as Bashan fears it, and unfortunately he got a taste of it oftener than Bashan ; for, first of all, I was younger and more hot-tempered during his epoch than I am at present, and secondly, his heedlessness often assumed a wanton and sinister aspect which simply clamoured for chastisement and urged me to it. When, driven to extremities, I would take down the whip from the nail, then, it is true, he would crawl under the table or bench and make himself small, but never a howl passed his lips when the blow, and perhaps yet another, came humming down upon his back; at most he gave a low moan, in case the whip bit too hard. But Bully Bashan begins to shriek and whimper when I merely raise my arm. In short, he is without pride or dignity, without self-restraint or self-discipline. But his activities seldom call for armed punitive intervention —the less so since I have long ago ceased to demand achievements from him which are contrary to his nature and insistence upon which might lead to a collision.

Tricks, for instance, I never expect from him—it would be futile. He is no savant, no market-place miracle-monger, no poodle-like valet—no professor—but a hunter-lad, full of go and vitality. I have already emphasised the fact that he is a splendid vaulter. If it be necessary, he will balk at no obstacle—if it be too high, he will simply take a running jump and climb over it, letting himself drop down on the other side—but take it he will. But the obstacle must be a *real* obstacle, that is, not one under which one may run or crawl; for then Bashan would consider it sheer insanity to jump over it. Such obstacles present themselves in the shape of a wall, a ditch, a barred gate, a fence without a hole. A horizontal bar, a stick held out, is no obstacle, and so, of course, one cannot well jump over it without bringing oneself into a silly contrariness to things as well as to one's reason. Bashan refuses to do this. He refuses. Should you attempt to persuade him to jump over some sham obstacle, you would finally in your wrath be forced to take him by the scruff of the neck and to hurl him over it, barking and yapping. He will hereupon assume a mien as though he had magnanimously permitted you to attain your wishes and will celebrate the result by caperings and rapturous barks. You may flatter him, beat him, but here you will encounter a resistance of sheer reason against the trick pure and simple which you will never be able to overcome.

He is not unobliging, gratifying his master means a great deal to him—he will vault over a hedge at my wish or command, and not only from his own impulses, and gladly will he reap his meed of praise and thanks for this. But even though you should beat him half to death, he will not jump over a pole or a stick, but run under it. He will beg a hundred times for forgiveness, for consideration, for mercy, for he fears pain, fears it, to the point of utter pusillanimity. But no fear and no pain can force him to do something which from a physical point of view would be mere child's play for him, but for which all mental capacities are obviously lacking in him. To demand this act of him is not to confront him with the question as to whether he should or should not jump—this question is already settled for him in advance, and the command simply means a clubbing. To demand the incomprehensible and therefore the impossible from him is, in his eyes, merely a pretext for a quarrel, for a disturbance of friendship and a chance to inflict a whipping, and is in itself the very inauguration of these things. This is Bashan's conception of things, as far as I can see, and I doubt whether one can speak of mere ordinary stubbornness in this connection. Obduracy may finally be broken, yes, it even demands to be broken, but Bashan would seal his refusal to perform a trick or feat with his very life.

A wondrous soul ! So friendly and intimate and yet so alien in certain traits, so alien that our language is incapable of doing justice to this canine logic. What relation has this, for instance, with that terrible circumstantiality, always so unnerving for the spectator, with which the meeting, the acquaintance or the mere recognition of dog and dog fulfil themselves ? My picaroon forays with Bashan have made me the

witness of hundreds of such meetings, or
rather I should say forced me to be an un-
willing, embarrassed witness.   And every
time, as long as the scene lasted, his usually
transparent behaviour became inscrutable
to me—I found it impossible to effect a
sympathetic penetration into the feelings,
laws, and tribal customs which form the
basis of his behaviour.   In reality the meeting
in the open of two dogs strange to each
other, belongs to the most poignant, arresting,
and pathetic of conceivable happenings.   It
takes place in an atmosphere of daemonry
and strangeness.   An inhibition operates
here for which there is no exacter term—
the two cannot pass each other—a terrible
embarrassment prevails.

I need scarcely speak of cases in which
the one party is locked inside some allot-
ment, behind a fence or a hedge—even then
it is not easy to see what humour the two
may be in, but the affair is comparatively
less ticklish.   They scent each other from

vast distances. Bashan suddenly appears at my side, as though seeking protection, and gives way to whimperings which proclaim an indefinite grief and perturbation of soul, whilst at the same time the stranger, the prisoner, starts up a furious barking, to which he seems anxious to give the character of vigilance energetically announcing itself, but which now and again impulsively reverts to tones which resemble those of Bashan's yearning, a tearfully jealous, a distressful whining. We approach the spot, drawing nearer and nearer. The strange dog has been awaiting us behind the fence—there he stands—scolding and lamenting his impotence, and makes wild leaps against the fence and pretends—no one can tell just how much he pretends—that he would infallibly tear Bashan to pieces, if he could but reach him. In spite of this, Bashan, who might easily remain at my side and walk past, goes towards the fence—he *must* go—he would go even contrary to my orders. Not to go would violate some immanent law—far more deeply-rooted, more inviolable than my own prohibition. So he walks up to the spot and, with a humble and inscrutable mien, fulfils that act of sacrifice which, as he well knows, always brings about a certain pacification and temporary reconciliation with the other dog— so long as he too performs the same act, even though it be in another spot and accompanied by low growlings and whines. Then both begin to chase wildly alongside the fence, the one on this, the other on the opposite side—dumb and always keeping parallel to each other. Both simultaneously face about at the end of the fence and race back towards the other end, turn about and race back once more. Suddenly, however, in the very middle, they remain as if rooted to the ground, no longer longitudinal to the fence—but at right angles with it, and touch noses through the rails. They stand thus for a considerable time, and then once

more resume their strange and ineffectual
race, shoulder to shoulder on either side
of the fence.   Finally, however, my dog
makes use of his liberty and races off.
This is always a terrible moment for the
imprisoned one.   This sudden lighting out
is to him something unendurable ; it is
villainy unutterable and unparalleled—to
think that the other dog, his racial colleague,
should really think of abandoning him !

So he raves, howls, acts like one possessed,
races up and down his territory, all by
himself, threatens to jump over the fence and
strangle the traitor, and keeps on hurling
the vilest curses after him.   Bashan cannot
help hearing all this pother, and he is most
disagreeably affected by it, as his guilty
and diffident air proclaims.   Still he refuses
to look back, and jogs easily along.   During
this the terrible maledictions to our rear
gradually decline in intensity and slowly
die away into low whinings and thin
yowls.

Such is the customary course of events
when one of the parties concerned happens
to be under duress. But the strange contrariety of things reaches its apex when the
rencontre takes place under equal conditions and both happen to be free of foot.
It is extremely unpleasant to be obliged to
describe this—really, it is the most oppres-
sive, embarrassing and ticklish situation conceivable. However——

Bashan, who has just been blithely gambolling about, comes to me, simply forcing
himself upon my attention with that peculiar
sniffling and whining which arise from the
very profounds of his nature. These sounds
cannot be interpreted as the expression of
any particular emotion, though I at once
recognise them as an attempt to tell me of
the approach of a strange dog. I peer
sharply about me. No mistake—there he
comes—and it is clear even from afar, as
proclaimed by his cautious and hesitant
advance, that he has become conscious of

the other. My own anxiety is scarcely less than that of the other two—I have premonitions that this meeting is going to be precarious and highly undesirable.

" Go 'way ! " I say to Bashan. " What d'ye mean by clinging to my leg ! Can't you two carry on negotiations amongst yourselves—and at a distance ? "

I try to push him away with my stick, for if it should come to a battle of bites, which—whether there be a reason for it or not—is extremely probable, it is sure to take place around my feet and I shall become the centre of a most unedifying tussle.

" Go 'way ! " I repeat hoarsely.

But Bashan does not go 'way. He continues to cling to me, tightly and helplessly. Only for a moment does he deign to move aside to sniff at a tree—an operation which the stranger, as I observe out of the corner of my eye, is also performing yonder. The distance between the two is now only twenty paces—the tension is fearful. The stranger has now assumed a crouching position like a tiger-cat, with head thrust forward, and in this highwaymanlike pose he awaits Bashan's approach, apparently in order to seize him by the throat at the proper moment. This, however, does not take place, nor does Bashan appear to expect it. At all events he continues to advance straight towards the lowering one, though with palpitant hesitancy and an alert though tragic mien. He would do so—would, in fact, be *forced* to do so, even though I were to leave him and pursue my path, abandoning him to all the perils of the situation. No matter how upsetting the *rencontre* may be, no thought can be given to evasion or escape. He goes as one that is under a spell—a ban. Both are bound to each other by some secret and tenebrous tie, and neither dares belie this. We have now approached within two paces.

And then the other dog gets up quietly, just as though he had never assumed the looks or attitude of a lion couchant and stands there precisely as Bashan stands—both with hangdog look, miserable and deeply embarrassed and both incapable of yielding an inch or of passing each other. They would like to be free of all this ; they turn away their heads, squint sadly aside. Thus they shove and slink towards each other, side by side, tense and full of a troubled watchfulness, flank to flank, and begin to snuffle at each other's hides.

It is during this procedure that the growlings begin. *Sotto voce*, I call Bashan by name and warn him, for this is the fateful moment which is to decide whether a tussle and biting-match is to take place, or whether I am to be spared this calamity. But the battle of bites, of tooth and claw, is upon us—in a flash—no one could say how or why. In a moment both of them are merely a tangle, a raving, chaotic tumult out of which arise horrible gutteral cries, as of dragons of the prime tearing each other.

In order to avert a tragedy I am forced
to interpose my stick, to seize Bashan by
his collar or by the scruff of his neck, and to
hoist him into the air with one arm with his
antagonist hanging to him with locked jaws
—or face whatever other terrors may be awaiting me—terrors which I am then fated to
feel in every nerve during the greater part
of the walk.   But it also happens that the
entire affair may pass off quite uneventfully,
and, as it were, ebb away.   Nevertheless, in
both contingencies it is difficult to get away
from the spot.   For even if these twain do
not happen to clamp themselves together by
the teeth, they remain fettered by a tenacious
inner bond.   In this case things proceed as
follows:—

You imagine that the two dogs have
already passed each other, for they are no
longer hesitating flank to flank, but are
aligned almost in keel formation, the one
with his head turned in one direction, the
other with his in the opposite direction.

They do not see each other ; they scarcely turn their heads, merely squinting towards the rear, straining the eyeball back as far as possible. Even though they are already separated by some short distance, the tenacious, sinister tie still holds and neither of them is sure whether the moment of liberation has arrived. Both would like to move off, but some inscrutable, conscientious anxiety prevents them from leaving the spot. Until at last—at last !—the ban is broken, and Bashan, redeemed, and with the air of having just been granted a new lease of life, goes bounding off.

I mention these things in order to indicate how strange and alien so close a friend may appear under certain circumstances—times when his entire nature reveals itself as something eerie and obscure. I brood upon this mystery and find no answer save a shake of the head. It is only by intuition and not by reason that I am able to identify myself with it. Otherwise I am well acquainted with Bashan's inner world, and am able to meet its every manifestation with sympathy and with cheerfulness—to understand his play of features, his whole behaviour.

How well, for example, a solitary example, do I know that chirruping yawn to which he has recourse whenever he has been disappointed in the results of a walk. It may be that the walk was all too short or else barren of events in a sporting sense—as sometimes happens when I have begun my day's work a little later than usual and have gone into the open air with Bashan for a brief quarter of an hour before sitting down at my desk. He walks beside me then, and yawns. It is a shameless, impolite, wide-angle yawning—the yawning of the beast, of the brute, and it is accompanied by a whistling, guttural note and by a hurt and bored look. It says, as clearly as words:—

" A nice sort of master I've got ! I went and fetched him from the bridge last night.

And now he goes and sits behind that there glass door, and I've got to wait till he goes out, and me a-perishing with impatience. And then at last when he *does* go out, he turns round again and starts back home before I've had a sniff at a single bit o' game ! A fine sort of master, eh ? And what a mean trick to play on a hound ! Why, he ain't fit to be called a master at all ! ''

Such are the sentiments expressed with rude clarity by these yawns of his—and there is no mistaking them. I am also aware that he is perfectly right in cherishing such sentiments and that in his eyes I am guilty. And so my hand steals towards his shoulder for a pat or two, or I proceed to stroke the top of his skull. But he has no use for caresses under such circumstances. He refuses to acknowledge or accept them. He gives another yawn, and this still more rudely than before, if that be possible, and withdraws himself from my conciliatory hand. He withdraws himself, even though he is extremely fond of such caresses, in accordance with his earthy, all too earthy sentimentality, and in contradistinction to the impervious Percy. He particularly appreciates being scratched upon the throat, and he has acquired a droll but adroit energy in guiding one's hand to the proper place by means of short movements of the head. That he ignores all tendernesses at present is due not only to his disillusion and disappointment, but also to the fact that he has no interest for such fondlings when in a state of movement, that is, a state of movement co-ordinated with mine. He is then obsessed by a masculine mood and spirit, and scorns all feminine touches. But an immediate change takes place as soon as I sit down. Then his heart expands and he becomes receptive to all friendly advances, and his manner of responding to them is full of rapturous and awkward insistence.

Often, when I chance to be seated on my chair in the angle of the garden wall or in

the grass with my back against some favourite
tree, reading a book, I am happy to interrupt
my literary occupation in order to speak
and play with Bashan. I repeat—to speak
with him. And what do I find to say? Well,
the conversation is usually limited to repeat-
ing his name to him—his name—those two
syllables which concern him more than all
others, since they designate nothing but
himself, and thus have an electrifying effect
upon his entire being. I thus stir and fire
his consciousness of his ego by abjuring him
in different tones and in different degrees
of emphasis to consider the fact that he is
called Bashan and that he *is* Bashan. By
keeping this up for a short time I am able
to throw him into a state of veritable ecstasy,
a kind of drunkenness of identity, so that
he begins to rotate upon his own axis and
to send loud barks towards heaven—all out
of sheer inner triumph and the proud com-
pulsion of his heart. Or we amuse each
other in that I flick him upon the nose,

whilst he snaps at my hand as at a fly. This forces both of us to laugh, yes, even Bashan must laugh. This laugh of his— to which I must instinctively respond, is for me the most wonderful and touching thing in the world. It is unutterably moving to see how his haggard canine cheek and the corners of his mouth quiver and jerk to the excitement of the teasing, how the dusky mien of the dumb creature takes on the physiognomic expression of human laughter, or how a troubled, helpless, and melancholy reflection of this appears and vanishes again to give way to the stigmata of fear and embarrassment, and then how it once more makes its wry appearance. . . .

But it is best to pause here and not involve myself deeper in detail. I must not allow my descriptions to exceed the limits which I have set. I merely wish to show my hero in all his glory and in his natural elements and in that position in life in which he is most himself and which casts the most favourable light upon his various gifts and accomplishments—that is to say, the hunt or chase. I must, however, as a preliminary, make the reader more closely acquainted with the scene of these joys—our hunting-grounds—my landscape along the river. For there is a strange affinity between this and the person of Bashan. This strip of land is as dear to me as it is to him—it is intimate and full of meaning—like himself. Therefore, without further ado or novellistic preciosity, let the following suffice in the way of description:—

THE HUNTING-GROUNDS

CHAPTER IV

THE HUNTING-GROUNDS

In the gardens of our small but spaciously arranged colony of villas there are huge trees—ancient giants which tower above the roofs. They offer a marked contrast to the tender saplings but recently planted. There can be no mistaking the fact that these trees are the original growth—the aboriginal inhabitants of this region. They are the pride and beauty of this still youthful settlement. They have been carefully preserved and tended—as far as this was possible. At those points where they happened to come into conflict with the surveyor's lines or with the fences dividing the various lots or tracts of land, that is to say, where some mossy, silvery, venerable trunk happened to be standing precisely on the lines of demarcation, you will find that the fence has made a little loop around the tree-trunk or that a gap has been left in the concrete of the garden wall. In these openings the Old Ones now tower, half privately, half publicly, their naked branches loaded with snow or bedizened with their small-leafed, late-sprouting foliage.

These trees are of the species of the ash—a tree which loves dampness as few others do. This quality at the same time offers a very significant commentary upon the essential peculiarity of our strip of country. It is not yet so very long ago that human ingenuity succeeded in turning it into something capable of cultivation and occupation—possibly a decade and a half ago—no longer. Before that it was a wilderness of swamps—a veritable brooding-place for gnats and mosquitoes—a waste in which willows, crippled poplars, and such-like gnarled and twisted arboreal stuff mirrored itself in stagnant pools. This region, you must know, is subject to inundation. A few metres under the surface there is a strata of water-tight soil. The ground has therefore always been swampy and water stood in every hollow. The draining of this fen was accomplished by lowering the surface of the river—I have no head for engineering, but some such expedient was made use of, with the result that the water which could not seep downward was induced to flow off laterally. Hence there are many subterranean brooks which pour themselves into the river at different spots. Solidity has thus been given to the soil, at least the greater part of it, for if you happen to know the district as Bashan and I know it, you would be able to discover in the thickets down-stream many a reedy sinkage which reminds you of pristine conditions. These are places of silence and secrecy, the damp coolth of which defies the hottest summer day, spots in which one is glad to rest and draw breath for a space.

The region really possesses its own peculiar

character and is to be distinguished at first
glance from the banks of the usual mountain
river with their pine woods and mossy
meadows. It has succeeded in retaining
this original peculiarity even since it has
come into the possession of the real estate
company. Even outside the gardens, the
aboriginal and original vegetation maintains
the upper hand over the imported and the
transplanted. It is true that in the avenues
and parks the horse-chestnut seems to thrive
as well as the swift-growing maple. Even
beeches and all kinds of decorative shrubbery
—but all these, including the alien poplar
which towers and ranges in rows of sterile
masculinity—are not native to the soil. I
said that the ash was an indigenous tree
here—it is to be found everywhere, and it
is of all ages—from giants hundreds of years
old to the soft shoots which, like so many
weeds, sprout in masses from the gravel.
It is the ash and its companions, the silver
poplar and the aspen, the birch and the

willow, both as a tree and a bush, which give distinctive character to this landscape. But these are all trees with small leaves, and this smallness and trimness of the foliage in conjunction with the frequently gigantic masses of the trees themselves, at once attract attention in this neighbourhood. The elm, however, is an exception, and we find it spreading its spacious leaves, fretted as by a jig-saw and shiny and sticky on their upper surface, to the sun. And everywhere there are great masses of creeping plants which weave themselves around the younger trunks in the woods and in a bewildering way entangle their leaves with these.

The slender alders form themselves into small groves in the hollows. The lime is scarcely to be met with at all, the oak never appears nor does the fir. Yet there are firs upon the eastern declivities which form the frontiers of our territory, for here the soil changes and with it the vegetation. There they rear black against the heavens and peer, sentinel-like, upon us in our lower levels.

From this bluff to the river is not more than a hundred metres—I have paced the distance. It may be that the strip of river-bank widens, fan-like, a little farther down-stream, but this divergence is in no way important. It is, however, remarkable what a diversity of landscape this limited region affords—even though one explore only the playground which lies along the river, explore it with restraint and moderation, like Bashan and myself. Our forays seldom exceed two hours, counting the advance and the retreat. The manifold nature of the views, however, and the fact that one is constantly able to change one's walks and to arrange combina-tions that are eternally new, without ever becoming bored with the landscape, is due to the circumstance that it is divided into three very different regions or zones. One may devote oneself separately to any of these or one may combine them by means of

slanting cross-paths. These three regions
are the region of the river and its immediate
bank on one side, the region of the bluff
on the other, and the region of the forest
in the middle.

The greater part of the breadth is occupied
by the zone of the forest, the willow brakes,
and the shrubbery of the bank—I find
myself hunting for a word which will more
perfectly fix and define this wonderful *terrain*
than the word wood, and yet I am unable
to find one. There can be no talk of a wood
in the usual sense of the term—a kind of
great pillared grove with moss and strewn
leafage and tree-trunks of fairly uniform
girth. The trees in our hunting-grounds
are of different ages and circumference.
Huge patriarchs of the willow and poplar
families are to be found among them,
especially along the river, though they are
also to be encountered in the inner woods.
Then there are others already full-grown
which might be ten or fifteen years old,

and finally a legion of thin stems—wild nurseries of nature's own crop of young ashes, birches, and elders. These do not, however, call forth any impression of meagreness, because, as I have already indicated, they are all thickly wrapped about with creepers. These give an air of almost tropical luxuriance to the whole. Yet I suspect that these creepers hinder the growth of their hosts, for during the years I have lived here, I do not remember having observed that any of these little stems had grown perceptibly thicker.

All trees belong to a closely-related species. The alder is a member of the birch family ; in the last analysis the poplar is nothing else than a willow. And one might even say that all of them approach the fundamental type of the latter. All foresters and woodmen know that trees are quite ready to accept a certain adaptation to the character of the circumjacent vicinity—a certain imitation or mimicry of the dominant taste in lines and forms. It is the fantastic, witch-like, distorted line of the willow which prevails here—this faithful companion and attendant of still and of flowing waters, with the crooked finger, projecting, broom-like, branching boughs, and it is these features which the others obviously seek to imitate. The silver poplar crooks herself wholly in the style of the willow, and it is often difficult to tell her from the birch which, seduced by the *genius loci*, also frequently affects the most extravagant crookednesses—though I would not go so far as to say that this dear and friendly tree was not to be found, and numerously found, in exceedingly shapely specimens. These, when the afternoon light is fervent and favourable, are even most enchanting to the eye.

The region knows it as a small silvery trunk with sparse single leaves in the crown, as a sweet grown-up limber virgin with the prettiest of chalky stems and a trim and languishing way of letting the locks of her foliage hang. But it also makes its appearance as a creature of absolutely elephantine proportions with a waist which no man could span with his arms and a rind which has preserved traces of its erstwhile whiteness only high up towards the top, whilst near the ground it has become a coarse, calcined and fissured bark.

As to the soil—this has little resemblance to that of a forest. It is pebbly, full of clay and even sand, and no one would dream of calling it fertile. And yet within limits it *is* fertile—even to luxuriance. A tall grass flourishes upon it, though this often assumes a dry, sharply angular and meagre character. In winter it covers the ground like trampled hay. Sometimes it degenerates into reeds, whilst in other parts it is soft, thick, and lush, mixed with hemlock, nettles, colt's foot, all manner of creeping, leafy stuff, high, rocket-like thistles, and young and tender tree-shoots. It is a favourite hiding-place for pheasants and quail, and the

vegetation runs in billows against the gnarled
boles of the tree-roots. Out of this chaos of
undergrowth and ground thicket the wild
vine and the wild hop-plant go gyrating up
in spirals, draping broad-leaved garlands
upon the trees and even in winter clinging
to the trunks with tendrils which resemble
hard and unbreakable wire.

This domain is neither forest nor park—
it is an enchanted garden—nothing less. I
will stoutly defend this term—even though
it refers to a poor, limited, and even crippled
bit of nature, the glories of which may be
exhausted with a few simple botanical names.
The ground is undulant ; it rises and falls
in regular waves. This feature gives a fine
completeness to the views—the eye is led
into the illimitable even at the sides. Yes,
even if this wood were to stretch for miles
to the right and left, even if it were to be
as broad as it is long, instead of merely
measuring a hundred and some odd paces
from the centre to the extreme edge on

either side, one could not feel more secluded, more lost, or isolated. Alone the ear is reminded by the regular and rushing sound of waters to the west that the river hovers within a friendly distance, near yet invisible. There are little gulches filled to the brim with bushes of elder, common privet, jasmine, and black elderberry, so that one's lungs on steamy June days are almost overcome by perfume. And then again there are sinkages in the ground—mere gravel-pits along the slopes and bottoms of which only a few willow shoots and a little dry sage manage to flourish.

All this has not ceased to exert a magic influence upon me, even though the place, for many a year, has been as a daily haunt to me. In some way I am fantastically moved and touched by all this, for example, by the massed foliage of the ash-trees, which reminds me somehow of the contours of huge bulls. These creeping vines and reedy thickets, this dampness and this drouth, this meagre jungle—to sum up my impressions as a whole—affect me a little like being transported to the landscape of another period of the Earth's growth, even to a submarine landscape—as though one were wandering at the bottom of the sea. This vision has a certain contact with reality, for water once stood or ran everywhere hereabout, especially in those seepages which have now assumed the shape of square meadow-basins surrounded by nurseries of ash-trees and serve sheep for drink and pasture. One of these ponds lies directly behind my house.

My delectable wilderness is criss-crossed by paths, by strips of trampled grass and also by pebbly trails. Obviously none of these were made, they simply grew through the agency of use. Yet no man could say by whom these paths have been trodden into the soil. It is only now and then, and usually as an unpleasant exception, that Bashan and I meet any one here. When such meetings do occur, my companion

comes to a sudden halt in startled surprise
and gives vent to a single muffled bark
which gives a pretty clear expression to my
own feelings in connection with the encounter. Even on fine sunny afternoons
in the summer, when great numbers of
pedestrians from the city come pouring into
the neighbourhood (it is always a few
degrees cooler here than elsewhere), we two
are able to wander quite undisturbed on the
inner ways. The public is apparently unaware of these, besides, the river is a great
attraction and draws them mightily. Hug-
ging its banks as closely as possible, that is,
when there is no flooding, the human river
wanders out into the countryside and then
comes rolling back in the evening. At most
we chance to stumble upon a pair of lovers
kissing in the bushes. With wide, shy, yet
insolent eyes, they regard us from their
bower, as though stubbornly bent on chal-
lenging us, daring us to say anything against
their being here, defying us to give any

open disapproval of their remote and guerilla love-making—intimations which we silently answer in the negative by beating a flank retreat, Bashan with that air of indifference with which all things that do not bear the scent of the wild about them affect him, and I with a perfectly inscrutable and expressionless face which allows no trace either of approval or disapproval to be seen.

But these paths are not the only means of traffic and communication in my domain. You will find *streets* there, or—to be more precise—preparations that may once have been streets, or were once destined to be such. It is like this: traces of the path-finding and path-clearing axe and of a sanguine spirit of enterprise in the realm of real estate reveal themselves for quite a distance beyond the built-up part of the country and the little villa colony. Some speculative soul had peered deeply into the untold possibilities of the future, and had proceeded upon a bold and audacious plan.

The society which had taken this tract of territory in hand some ten or fifteen years before had cherished plans far more magnificent than those which came to pass, for originally the colony was not to have been confined to the handful of villas which now stand there. Building lots were plentiful, for more than a mile down-stream everything had been prepared, and is no doubt still prepared for possible buyers and for lovers of a settled suburban manner of life.

The councils of this syndicate had been dominated by large and lofty ideals. They had not contented themselves with building proper jetties along the banks, with the creation of riverside walks and quays and with the planting of parks and gardens. They had gone far beyond all this, the hand of cultivation had invaded the woods themselves, had made clearings, piled up gravel, united the wilderness by means of streets, a few lengthwise and still more crosswise. They are well-planned and handsome streets,

or sketches of streets, in coarse macadam,
with the hint of a curb and roomy sidewalks.
On these, however, no one goes walking
but Bashan and myself—he upon the good
and durable leather of his four paws—I upon
hob-nailed boots, because of the macadam.

The villas which should long ago have
risen hospitably along these streets, according
to the calculations and intentions of the
society, have, for the present, refused to
materialise, even though I have set so
excellent an example as to build my own
house in these parts. They have remained
absent, I say, for ten, for fifteen years, and
so it is small wonder that a certain dis-
couragement has settled down upon the
neighbourhood, and that a disinclination for
further expenditures and for the completion
of that which was so magnificently begun,
should make itself felt in the bosom of the
society.

Everything had progressed admirably up
to a certain point. Things had even gone

so far as the christening of the new streets.
For these thoroughfares without inhabitants
have right and regular names, just like
ordinary or orthodox streets in the city or
in the civilised suburbs. But I would give
much to know what dreamy soul or retro-
spective "highbrow" of a speculator had
assigned them. There is a Goethe and a
Schiller, a Lessing and a Heine Street—there
is even an Adalbert Stifter Street upon which
I stroll with particular sympathy and reverence in my hob-nailed boots. Square stakes
are visible, such as may be seen in at the
corners of the raw and uncompleted streets
in the suburbs where there are no corner
houses. Little blue enamelled shields with
white letters are fastened to these stakes.
These shields, alas, are not in the best
condition. They have stood here far too
long, giving a name to adumbrations of
streets in which no one cares to live, and they
have been singled out to bear the stigmata
of disappointment, fiasco, and arrested

development to which they give public
expression. They are wrapped in an air
of forlorn disquietude and neglect. Nothing
has been done for their upkeep nor for their
renewal, and the weather and the sun have
played havoc with them. The enamel, to
a great extent, has split and cracked off,
the white letters have been eaten away by
rust, so that in place of their smooth and
glittering whiteness there are only brown
spots and gaps with hideous, jagged edges—
disfigurements which tear the image of the
name asunder and often render it illegible.

One of these blue enamelled signboards
imposed a tremendous strain upon my intel-
lect when I first came hither and penetrated
this region on my tours of exploration. It
was a signboard particularly long in shape
and the word street (*strasse*) had been
preserved without a break. But of the
actual name which, as I have indicated,
was very long, or rather had been very
long, the letters were nearly all completely

" blinded " or devoured by rust. The
reddish-brownish gaps gave one some idea
of their number, but nothing was decipher-
able except the half of a capital S and an e
in the middle, and another e at the end.
This riddle was a little too much for my
astuteness—I was face to face with too many
unknown quantities. So I stood there for
a long time, my hands upon my back,
staring at the long signboard and studying
it closely. And then I gave it up and went
strolling along the rudimentary pavement
with Bashan. But whilst I thought that I
was occupying myself with other things,
this particular thing kept working within
the mnemonic depths of me. My sub-
intelligence kept scenting out the destroyed
name, and suddenly it shot into my consciousness. I stood still—as in a fright. I
rushed back and once more planted myself
in front of the signboard. I counted and
compared and tested the elements of my
guess. Yes, it fitted, it " worked out ! "

We were wandering in the street which had been called " Shakespeare."

These signboards befit the streets which justify their metallic existence, and these streets the signboards which give them a local habitation and a name. Both of them are dreamily and wonderfully lapped in forgetfulness and decay. They pursue their way through the wood which they have invaded—but the wood refuses to rest. It refuses to leave these streets inviolate for a decade or more until settlers choose to pitch their tents or villas here. So the wood calmly goes to work and makes preparations to close the streets, for the green things that grow here have no fear of gravel or macadam —they are used to it and thrive in it and on it. So everywhere upon the streets and upon the pavements the purple-headed thistles, the blue sage, silvery willow shrubs, and the green of young ash-tree sprouts begin to take root and shoot forth.

There can be no doubt—these park-like

streets with the poetic names are running wild—the jungle is once more devouring them. Whether one be disposed to lament the fact or rejoice over it—it is certain that in another ten years the Goethe, Schiller, and Heine Streets will no longer be passable, and will very likely have vanished utterly. At present, to be sure, there is no cause for complaint. Surely, from a pictorial and romantic point of view, there are no lovelier streets in all the world than precisely these in precisely their present condition. Nothing could be more grateful to the soul than to ramble through this negligence, this incompleteness—that is, when one is well and sturdily shod and need not fear the coarse gravel. It is edification to the spirit to survey the manifold wild vegetation of the tract and the groves of tiny-leafed trees fettered by their soft dampness—sweet glimpses which frame and shut in these perspectives. Just such a group of trees was painted three hundred years ago by that great master of landscapes—he who came out of Lorraine. But what am I saying ?—*such* as he painted ? It was this one—and none other—which he painted. He was here ; he knew the region, and if that rhapsodical member of the real estate company who christened the streets in my park had not so rigidly restricted himself to literature, then one or the other of these rust-corroded signs might well cause me to guess at the name of Claude Lorraine.

I have now described the region of the central wood. But the sloping land towards the east also possesses charms which are not to be despised, at least so far as Bashan and myself are concerned, and for reasons which will be revealed later. One might also call it the zone of the brook, for it is a brook which gives it an idyllic landscape quality. With the charm of its banks of forget-me-nots it forms a counterpart on the hitherside to the zone of the puissant river yonder— the roar and rushing turbulence of which one is still able to hear in this spot—but only very faintly and softly and only when the west wind is blowing. There where the first cross street, running from the avenue of poplars between the meadow ponds and the clumps of trees towards the slope, debouches at the foot of this slope, there is a path that leads towards the left. This is used in winter-time as a bob-sled run by the youth of the region, and slants towards the lower-lying levels.

Where the run becomes level the brook begins its course, and it is here that master and dog love to amble beside it on the right bank or the left—which again affords variety—and also to make excursions along the slope with its variegated configuration. To the left extend meadows studded with trees. A country nursery lies not far away and reveals the back of its farm buildings. Sheep are usually at pasture here, cropping the clover. They are under the chairmanship—so to speak—of a not very clever little girl in a red frock. This little girl seems to suffer from a veritable passion to rule and command. She is constantly crouching low, propping her hands upon her knees and shouting with all her might in a cacophonous voice. And yet she is horribly afraid of the ram, who takes on huge and majestic proportions on account of the thickness of his wool and who refuses to be bullied and does whatever he pleases.

Whenever Bashan's appearance causes a panic among the sheep, the child invariably raises its hideous outcry, and these panics occur quite regularly and quite contrary to Bashan's intentions—for, if you could peer into his inmost soul, you would discover that sheep are a matter of absolute indifference to him. He treats them like so much empty air, and by his indifference and his scrupulous and even contemptuous carefulness he even seeks to prevent the outbreak of the dunderheaded hysteria which dominates their ranks. Though their scent is certainly strong enough for my own nostrils (yet not unpleasantly so), it is not the scent of the wild that emanates from them, and so Bashan, of course, has not the slightest interest in hounding them. Nevertheless, a simple sudden motion on his part, or even his mere shaggy appearance, is sufficient to cause the whole herd, which but a moment ago was peacefully grazing, widely separated and bleating in the quavering treble of the lambs and in the deeper contralto and bass of the ewes and the ram, to go storming off in a solid mass neck and neck, whilst the stupid child, crouching low, shouts after them until her voice cracks and her eyes pop out of her head. Bashan, however, looks up at me as much as to say: Judge for yourself whether *I* am to blame. Have *I* given them any cause for this?

On one occasion, however, something quite contrary happened, something perverse and incomprehensible—something still more extraordinary and unpleasant than the panic.

One of the sheep, quite an ordinary specimen of its kind, of average size and average sheepish visage, with a small upward curving mouth which appeared to smile and gave an expression of almost mocking stupidity to its face, seemed to be spellbound and fascinated by Bashan and came to join him. It simply followed him—detached itself from the herd, left the pasture and clung to Bashan's heels, quietly smiling in exaggerated foolishness, and following him whithersoever he turned. He left the path—the sheep did likewise; he ran and it followed at a gallop ; he stood still, and it stood still—immediately behind him and smiling its mysterious Mona Lisa smile.

Displeasure and embarrassment became visible in Bashan's face. The situation into which he had been plunged was really ridiculous. There was neither sense nor significance in it—neither in a good or a bad sense. The whole thing, confound it— was simply preposterous—nothing of the

kind had ever happened to him—or to me.
The sheep went farther and farther from
its basis, but this did not seem to trouble it
in the least. It followed the discomfited and
irritated Bashan farther and farther, visibly
determined not to separate from him ever
again, but to follow him whithersoever he
might go. He remained close beside me,
not so much out of fear, since there was no
occasion for this, as out of shame at the
dishonour of the situation in which he found
himself. Finally, as though his patience
were at an end, he stood still, turned his head,
and growled ominously. This caused the
sheep to bleat, and its bleating sounded like
the wicked laughter of a human being, which
so terrified poor Bashan that he ran away
with his tail between his legs—and the sheep
straight after him, with comic jumps and
curvetings.

We were already at a considerable distance
from the herd. In the meantime the half-
witted little girl was screaming as though

she would burst, still crouching and bending
upon her knees and even drawing these up
as high as her face, so that from a distance
she looked like a raving and malformed
gnome. And then a farm-maid, with an
apron over her skirts came running up,
either in answer to the cries of the obsessed
little one or because she had noticed the
happenings from afar. She came running,
I say, with a pitchfork in one hand. With
the other she supported her bodice, which,
I surmise, was unsupported and which was
visibly disposed to shake a trifle too violently
as she ran. She came up panting and at
once proceeded to shy the sheep, which was
slowly pacing along, like Bashan himself,
into the proper direction with the fork,
though without success. The sheep, it is
true, sprang aside with a swift flank movement, but in an instant it was once more on
Bashan's trail. Nothing seemed to be able
to induce it to give up.

I then realised that the only thing to do

was to turn tail myself, and so I turned round. We all retraced our steps, Bashan at my side, behind him the sheep, and behind the sheep the maid with the pitch-fork, whilst the child in the red frock kept on yelling and stamping. It was not enough, however, that we should go back as far as the herd—it was necessary to finish the job and to proceed to the final destination. We were obliged to enter the farmyard and then the sheep-stable with the broad sliding-door which the maid with muscular arm rolled to one side before us. We thereupon marched in, and after we were all inside, we three were forced to make a swift and adroit escape so as to be able to shove the stable door to before the very nose of the beguiled sheep, making it a prisoner. It was only after this operation had been gone through that Bashan and I were able to resume our interrupted promenade amidst the fervent thanks of the maid. During the entire walk, however, Bashan persisted in maintaining a humble and disconsolate air.

So much for the sheep. Closely adjacent to the farm buildings on the left there is an extensive colony of small market-gardens. These are owned and tended by the clerks and working men of the city, and are the source of much joy, exercise, and considerable supplies of cheap flowers and vegetables. The gardens have a cemetery-like effect with their many arbours and summer houses, built in imitation of tiny chapels and with their countless small, fenced-in plots. The whole is enclosed by a wooden fence with an ornamental gateway. No one, however, except the small amateur gardeners, is permitted to have admittance through this wooden grille. At times I see some bare-armed man there digging up his little vegetable garden, a square rod or so in size, and always it seems to me as though he were digging his own grave. Beyond these gardens lie open meadows which are covered with

mole-hills and which extend to the edge of
the central wooded region. Here, in addition
to the mole-hills, there are also great numbers
of field-mice—a fact which must be solemnly
remarked in view of Bashan and his multi-
form joy in the chase.

On the other side, that is to say, to the
right, the brook and the slope continue—
the latter, as I have already indicated, in
diverse configuration. At first, covered with
fir-trees, it displays a dusky and sunless
visage. Later it transforms itself to a sand-
pit which warmly refracts the beams of the
sun ; still later it converts itself into a gravel-
pit, and then to a cataract of bricks—just
as though a house had been demolished
higher up and the débris hurled down the
slope. This has imposed temporary difficulties upon the course of the brook. But
the brook rises equal to the occasion ; its
waters mount a trifle and spread themselves
out, stained red by the dust of the broken
brick and also discolouring the grass along

the bank. After this they flow the clearer and the more gaily on their way with glistenings here and there upon the surface.

I have a great love for brooks, as I have for all bodies of water—from the ocean to the smallest, scum-covered puddle. When I happen to be in the mountains during the summer and chance to hear the secret splashing and gossip of such a streamlet, then I must follow the liquid call, even though it be distant, and I cannot rest until I have found its hiding-place. Then, face to face, I make acquaintance with the talkative child of the crags and the heights. Beautiful are the proud torrential brooks which come down in crystalline thunder between pines and steep terraces of stone, form green, ice-cold pools in rocky baths and basins, and then go plunging to the next step in a dissolution of snowy foam. But I am also fond of looking upon the brooks of the flatland, whether they be shallow, so as scarcely to cover the polished, silvery, and slippery pebbles of their beds, or as deep as little rivers which—protected on both banks by low, overhanging willows—go shoulder-ing themselves forward with a vigorous thrust, flowing more swiftly in the middle than at the sides.

Who, being free to make his choice, would not follow the course of the waters on his wanderings? The attraction which water exercises upon the normal man is natural and mystically sympathetic. Man is a child of water. Our bodies are nine-tenths water, and during a stage of our pre-natal development, we even have gills. As for myself, I gladly confess that the contemplation of water in every shape and form is for me the most immediate and poignant joy in nature—yes, I will even go so far as to say that true abstractedness, true self-forgetfulness, the real merging of my own circumscribed existence in the universal, is granted to me only when my eyes lose themselves in some great liquid mirror. Thus, in the face of the sleeping or the charging and crashing of the on-rushing sea, I am like to be transported into a condition of such profound and organic dreams, of such a remote absence from myself, that all sense of time is lost and tedium becomes a thing without meaning, since hour upon hour spent in such identification and communion melt away as though they were but minutes. But I also love to lean upon the rail of a bridge that crosses a brook, and remain fixed to it as with thongs, losing myself in the vision of the flowing, streaming and whirling element—quite immune to the fear or impatience with which I ought to be filled in view of that other streaming and flowing that goes on about me—the swift, fluid flight of time. Such love of the water, and all that water means, renders the tight little territory which I inhabit the more important and precious to me in that it is surrounded on both sides by water.

The local brook is of the simple and faithful species. There is nothing very remarkable about it—its character is based upon friendly averages. It is of a naiveté as clear as glass, without subtlety or deception, without an attempt to simulate depth by means of murkiness. It is shallow and clear and quite innocently reveals the fact that its bottom harbours castaway tin pots and the carcass of a lace-boot in a coat of green slime. It is, however, deep enough to serve as a habitation to pretty, silvery-gray and extremely nimble little fish, which, I presume, are minnows and which dart away in wide zigzag lines at our approach. My brook widens here and there into ponds with fine willows along the edges. One of these willows I always regard lovingly as I pass by. It grows—I had almost said she grows—close to the bluff, and thus at some distance from the water. But it stretches one of its boughs longingly towards the brook and has really succeeded in reaching the flowing water with the silvery foliage that plumes the tip of this bough. There it stands, with fay-like fingers wet in the stream and draws pleasure from the contact.

It is good to walk here, lightly assailed by the warm summer wind. The weather is warm, so it is probable that Bashan will go wading into the brook to cool his belly— only his belly, for he has a distinct aversion to bringing the more elevated parts of his anatomy in contact with the water. There he stands, with his ears laid back and an expression of piety and alertness upon his face, and lets the water swirl around him and past him. After this he comes sidling up to me in order to shake himself—an operation which, according to his own conviction, must occur in my immediate vicinity. The vigour with which he shakes himself causes a thin spray of water and mud to fly my way. It is no use warding him off with flourished stick and intense

objurgations. Under no conditions will he
tolerate any interference with anything that
appears to him natural, inevitable, and
according to the fitness of things.

Farther on the brook, in pursuing its
course towards the setting sun, reaches a
small hamlet which commands a view towards
the north—between the woods and the slope
—and at the entrance to this hamlet lies the
tavern. Here the brook once more broadens
into a pond. The women of the village kneel
at the edge of this and wash their linen. A
little foot-bridge crosses the stream. Should
you venture over you will set foot upon a
road which leads from the village towards
the city, running between the edge of the
wood and the edge of the meadow. Should
you leave this road on the right you would
be able to reach the river in a few steps by
means of a wagon-road that cuts through the
wood.

We are now within the zone of the river.
The river itself lies before us green and

streaked with white and full of liquid roar-
ings. It is actually only a great mountain
torrent. Its everlasting rushing sound can
be heard with a more or less muffled rever-
beration everywhere throughout the region.
Here it swells and crashes overwhelmingly
upon the ears. It might, in fact, serve as
a substitute for the sacred and sounding
onset of the sea—if no sea is to be had.
The ceaseless cry of innumerable land-gulls
intermingles with the voice of the stream.
In autumn and in winter, and even during
the spring, these gulls go circling round and
round the mouths of the overflow-pipes,
filling the air with their screams. Here they
find their food until the season grows milder
and permits them to make their way to the
lakes in the hills—like the wild and half-
wild ducks which also spend the cool and
the cold months in the vicinity of the city,
balance themselves on the waves, permit
themselves to be carried by the current
which turns them round and rocks them at

will, and then just at the moment when some rapid or whirlpool threatens to engulf them, fly up with light and vibrant wing and settle down once more upon the water —a little farther up-stream.

The region of the river is arranged and classified as follows:—close to the edge of the wood there stretches a broad level of gravel. This is a continuation of the poplar avenue which I have mentioned so frequently, and runs, say, for about a kilometre down-stream, that is to say, to the little ferryman's house—of which more anon. Behind this the thicket comes closer to the river channel. The purpose of this desert of gravel is clear ; it is the first and most prominent of the longitudinal streets, and was lavishly planned by the real estate company as a charming and picturesque esplanade for elegant turn-outs—with visions of gentlemen on horse-back approaching spick-and-span landaus and victorias glistening in their enamel and engaging in delicate badinage with smiling and "beauteous" ladies reclining at ease under dainty parasols.

Close to the ferryman's house there is a huge signboard in a state of advanced decrepitude. This proclaims what was to have been the immediate goal, the temporary termination of the carriage *corso*. For there in broad and blatant letters you may read that this corner site is for sale for the erection of a park café and a fashionable refreshment "establishment." Well, the purpose remains unfulfilled, and the building site is empty. For in place of the park café, with its little tables, its hurrying waiters, and glass-and-cup sipping and straw-sucking guests, there is only the big wooden signboard—aslant—a resigned, collapsing bid without a bidder, and the corso itself only a waste of coarsest gravel, covered with willow bushes and with blue sage almost as thickly as the Goethe or Lessing Streets.

Alongside the esplanade, nearer to the river, there runs a smaller gravel way which is also overgrown with insurgent shrubbery. It is characterised by grass mounds which arise at intervals and from which telegraph-poles mount into the air. Yet I am fond of frequenting this road on my walks, first because of the change, and second because the gravel permits of clean though somewhat difficult locomotion, when the clayey footpath yonder does not appear passable during days of heavy rain. This footpath, actually the real promenade, runs for miles along the river and then finally degenerates into wild, haphazard trails along the bank. It is lined along the riverside with saplings, maple and birch, and on the land side it is flanked by the mighty primitive inhabitants of the region—willows, aspens, and silver poplars—all of them colossal in their dimensions. The escarpment plunges steeply and sheerly towards the river-bed. It is protected by ingenious works of woven willow-withes and by a concrete armour along its lower parts against the mounting flood water which once or twice a year comes rolling hither—when the snows melt in the mountains or the rain overdoes itself. Here and there the slope hospitably offers one the use of wooden steps, half ladders and half stairs, by means of which one may, with a fair degree of comfort, descend into the actual river-bed, which is usually quite dry. It is the reserve gravel bed of the big wild brook, and is about six metres wide.

The stream behaves like all other members of its family, the small as well as the smallest, that is to say, according to the weather and the water conditions in the upper mountain regions. Sometimes its course will be a mere green flowing tunnel with the rocks scarcely covered and with the gulls appearing to stand stilt-legged on the very surface itself. And then, again, it will assume a most formidable character, swelling into a wide stream, filling its bed with gray watery fury and tumult, and bearing along in its headlong course all kinds of unseemly objects such as old baskets, pieces of wooden crates, bushes, and dead cats in its circling wrath, and showing a great disposition to flooding and to deeds of violence.

The reserve or overflow channel is also armoured against high water by the same parallel, slanting, and hurdle-like arrangements of willow branches. It is covered with beach-grass and wild oats as well as with the show-plant of the neighbourhood, the dry, omnipresent blue sage. It offers good walking, thanks to the strip of quay formed of tooled and even stone, which runs along the extreme limit of the water. This gives me a further, and in fact favourite, possibility of adding variety to my promenades.

It is true that the unyielding stone is not particularly good going, but one is fully recompensed by the intimate proximity of the water. Then one is also able now and then to walk in the *sand* beside the quay. Yes, there is real sand there between the

gravel and the beach-grass, sand that is a
trifle mixed with clay and not so sacredly
pure as that of the sea, but nevertheless real
sand that has been washed up. I am thus
able to fancy myself strolling upon a real
strand down there, inscrutably drawing my
foot along the perilous edge of the salt
flood. There is no lack of surgings, even
if there is of surges, nor of the clamour of
gulls, nor of that kind of space-anni-
hilating monotony which lulls one into a
sort of narcotic absentmindedness. The
level cataracts are rushing and roaring all
around, and halfway to the ferryman's house-
the voice of a waterfall joins the chorus—
from over yonder where the canal, debouch-
ing at a slant, pours itself into a river. The
body of this fall is arched, smooth, glassy
like that of a fish, and an everlasting boiling
tumult goes on at its base.

It is beautiful here when the sky is blue
and the flat ferry decorated with a pennant
in honour of the weather or some other

festival occasion. There are other boats in this spot, but the ferry is fastened to a wire rope which in turn is fastened to another and thicker wire cable. This is stretched across the river in such a way as to let a pulley run along it. The current itself furnishes the motive power for the ferry-boat and a pressure from the ferryman's hand upon the rudder does the rest. The ferryman lives in the ferry-house with his wife and child, and this house lies a short distance from the upper footpath. It has a little garden and a hen-house, and is evidently an official dwelling and therefore rent-free. It is a kind of villa of liliputian proportions, lightly and whimsically built with little bays and gables, and appears to boast of two rooms below and two above. I love to sit on the bench in front of the garden close to the upper footpath. Bashan then squats upon my foot ; the hens of the ferryman amble about me and give their heads a forward jerk with every step. And usually the cock comes to perch upon the back of the bench and lets the green Bersaglieri feathers of his tail hang down behind, sitting beside me thus and measuring me luridly from the side with his red eye.

I watch the traffic on the ferry. It could scarcely be called strenuous, nor even lively, for it consummates itself, at large and liberal intervals. So I find all the more pleasure in the scene when a man or a woman with a market-basket appears on the farther bank and demands to be carried across the river. For the poetic element in that fine call, "Ferry ahoy!" remains full of human captivation as in ancient days, even though the action fulfils itself, as here, in new and progressive forms. Double steps of wood for the coming and the departing traveller lead down the escarpment on both sides into the bed of the river and to the landing-places. And on both sides there is an electric button affixed to the rail.

A man appears on the other bank, stands

still and peers across the water. No longer,
however, as in former times, does he hollow
his hands into a trumpet and shout through
them. He walks towards the push-button,
stretches out his arms and performs a slight
pressure with his thumb. There is a clear,
thin tinkle in the house of the ferryman.
This is the modern " Ferry ahoy ! " and
it is poetic even thus. There stands the
prospective passenger and watches and waits.
And almost at the very moment at which
the bell tinkles, the ferryman comes out of
his little house, just as though he had stood
or sat behind the door, merely waiting for
the signal. The ferryman, I repeat, comes
out—and in his walk there is something
which suggests that he has been set in
motion directly by the pressure upon the
push button—just as one may shoot at a
door in a tiny hut among the targets in the
shooting-galleries. If you chance to make
a bull's-eye, it flies open and a tiny figure
comes out—say a milkmaid or a soldier.

Without showing the slightest sign of undue haste the ferryman walks with swinging arms through his little garden, crosses the footpath, descends the wooden steps to the river, pushes off the ferry, and holds the rudder whilst the pulley runs along the taut wire, and the boat is driven across by the current. The boat bumps against the other bank ; the stranger jumps in ; upon reaching the hither bank he hands the ferryman a nickel coin and leaps up the wooden steps with alacrity. He has conquered the river, and turns either to the right or to the left. Sometimes when the ferryman is prevented from being at his post, either through illness or more urgent household affairs, then his wife or even his child will come out of the house and fetch the stranger across. They are able to perform this office as well as he—even I could attend to it. The job of the ferryman is an easy one and requires no special capacity or training. Surely he is a lucky man, this

ferrymaster, in having such a job and being
able to live in the neat dwarf villa. Any fool
would at once be able to step into his place,
and the knowledge of this keeps him modest
and grateful. On the way back to his
house he greets me very politely (with
Grüss Gott) as I sit there on the wooden
bench between the dog and the rooster.
It is clear that he wishes to remain on a good
footing with every one.

A smell of tar, a wind brushing across the
waters, and a plashing sound against the
wooden sides of the boats. What more
could I desire? Sometimes I am seized by
another memory of home. It comes upon
me when the water is deep and still and
there is a somewhat musty odour in the air,
and then these things take me back to the
Laguna, back to Venice, where I spent so
many years of my youth. And then again
there is storm and there is flood, and the everlasting rain comes pouring down. Wrapped
in a rubber coat, with wet and streaming

face, I brace myself against the stiff west
wind along the upper way, a wind that
tears the young poplars from their poles
and makes it clear why the trees here incline
away from the west and have crowns which
grow only from one side of the branches.
When we go walking in rains such as these,
Bashan frequently stands still and shakes
himself so that he is the dark centre of a
dull, gray flurry of water. The river at
such times is a different river. Swollen,
murky-yellow, it comes rolling on, wearing
upon its face an ominous catastrophic look.
This storm-flood is full of a lurching, crowd-
ing, tremendous haste, an insensate hurry.
It usurps the entire reserve channel up to
the very edge of the escarpment, and leaps
up against the concrete walls, the protective
works of willow boughs, so that one involuntarily utters thanks to the wise forethought
which established these defences. The eerie
thing about these flood-waters is that the
river grows quiet, much quieter than usual,

in fact it becomes almost silent. The customary surface rapids are no longer visible; the stream rolls too high for these. But the spots where these rapids were, are to be recognised by the deeper hollows and the higher waves, and by the fact that the crests of these waves curl over backwards and not forwards—like the waves of the current. The waterfall no longer plays a part, its glistening curved body is now flat and meagre, and the pother at its base has vanished through the height of the water level.

So far as Bashan is concerned, his astonishment at such a change in the aspect of things is beyond expression. He remains in a state of constant amazement. He is unable to realise that the places in which he has been accustomed to trot and run should have vanished, should have utterly vanished —think of it!—and that there should be nothing there but water—water! In his fright he scampers up the escarpment in a

kind of panic—away from the plunging,
spattering flood and looks around at me
with waggings of his tail, after which he
casts further dubious glances at the water.
A kind of embarrassment comes upon him
—and he gives way to a trick of his—opening
his mouth obliquely and thrusting his tongue
into the corners—a play of feature which
affects one as being as much human as it is
animal. As a means of expression it is
somewhat unrefined and subservient, but
thoroughly comprehensible. The whole
effect is about the same as would be conveyed
by a rather simple-minded yokel in the face
of an awkward situation, provided he went
so far as to scratch his head as Bashan
scratches his neck.

Having occupied myself in some detail
with the zone of the river, and described the
whole region, I believe that I have succeeded
in giving my readers a picture of it. I
rather like my own description of the place,
or rather the place as presented in my

description, but I like it still better as a piece of nature. For there is no doubt that as a piece of living nature, it is still more diversified and vivid, just as Bashan himself is in reality warmer, more lively and lovable than in this counterfeit presentment. I am attached to this stretch of landscape and grateful to it, and so I have described it with something of the meticulosity with which the old Dutch masters painted. It is my park and my solitude, and it is for this reason that I have sought to conjure it up before the reader's eye. My thoughts and my dreams are mingled and intergrown with its scenes, like the leaves of its creepers with the stems of its trees.

I have looked upon it at all hours and at all seasons ; in autumn when the chemical smell of the fading leaves fills the air, when the white legions of the thistle-down have all been blown to the winds, when the great beeches of the *Kurgarten* spread a rust-coloured carpet of leaves about them on the

meadows, and when afternoons dripping
with gold merge into theatrically romantic
twilights with the crescent moon swimming
in the skies, with a milky brew of mist
hovering over the levels and the afterglow
of the sunset smouldering through the black
silhouettes of the trees. And also in winter
when all the gravel is covered with snow
and soft and smooth, so that one may walk
upon it in one's rubber overshoes, and when
the river goes shooting black between the
pale frost-bound shores and the cry of
hundreds of fresh-water gulls fills the air
from morning to evening. Nevertheless the
easiest and most familiar intercourse with
this landscape is during the mild months,
when no special equipment in the way of
defensive clothing is necessary, and one may
go for a quick stroll for a quarter of an hour,
betwixt and between two showers of rain,
and, in passing, bend aside the branch of a
black alder tree and cast a look into the
wandering waves. It is possible that visitors

have been to call upon me, and I have been
left behind, stranded, as it were, within my
own four walls, crushed by conversation,
and with the breath of the strangers apparently still hanging in the air. It is good then
to go at once and loaf for a little along the
Heine or Schiller Street, to draw a breath
of fresh air and to anoint myself with
Nature. I look up to the heavens, peer
into the green depths of the world of tender
and delicate leaves, my nerves recover themselves and grow quiet—peace and serenity
return to my spirit.

Bashan is always with me on such forays.
He had not been able to prevent an invasion
of the house by the outer world in the shape
of the visitors, even though he had lifted
up his voice in loud and terrible protest.
But that had done no good, and so he had
stepped aside. And now he is jubilant that
he and I are once more together in the
hunting-grounds. With one ear turned
carelessly inside out, and loping obliquely,

as is the common habit of dogs—that is, with his hind legs moving not directly behind his front legs, but somewhat to the side, he goes trotting on the gravel in front of me. And suddenly I see that some tremendous emotion has seized him, body and soul. His short bobbed tail begins to wave furiously. His head lunges forward and to one side, his body stretches and extends itself. He jumps hither and thither, and the next moment, with his nose still glued to the ground, he goes darting off. He has struck a scent. He is on the spoor of a rabbit.

THE CHASE

CHAPTER V

THE CHASE

THE region is rich in game, and so we go a-hunting it. That is to say, Bashan goes hunting and I look on. In this wise we hunt : rabbits, quail, field-mice, moles, ducks and gulls. But we do not by any means fight shy of bigger game ; we also track pheasants and even deer—whenever such first-rate quarry—as sometimes happens— strays into our hunting-grounds. This always furnishes an exciting spectacle—when the long-legged, lightly-built animal, the furtive deer, all yellow against the snow and with its white-tufted hindquarters bobbing, goes flying before little old Bashan who is straining every nerve. I follow the course of events with the greatest interest and tension. It is not as if anything were ever to result from this chase, for that has never happened and never will happen. But the lack of tangible results does not in the least diminish either Bashan's joy or his passion for hunting, nor does it in any way minimise my pleasure. We pursue the chase for its own sake and not for the sake of prey or booty or any other utilitarian purpose.

Bashan, as I have said, is the active member. He does not expect any save a moral support from me, since no personal and immediate experience has taught him a more pronounced and practical manner of co-operation. I lay particular stress upon the words " personal " and " immediate," for it is more than probable that his ancestors, in so far as they belonged to the tribe of setters, were familiar with more actual methods of hunting. On occasion I have asked myself whether some memory of this might not survive in him and whether this could not be aroused by some accidental impulse. It is certain that on Bashan's plane of existence the life of the individual is less differentiated from the species than in our case. Birth and death signify a far less profound vacillation of the balance of being ; perhaps the inheritances of the blood are more perfectly preserved, so that it would merely be an *apparent* contradiction to speak of inborn experiences, unconscious memories which, once aroused, would be able to confuse the creature in the matter of its own personal experiences and cause it to be dissatisfied with these. I once courted this thought, but then rid myself of it, just as Bashan had obviously rid himself of the thoughts of the brutal incident of which he had been a witness and which gives me occasion for these deliberations.

When I go forth to hunt with him, it usually chances to be noon—half-past eleven or twelve o'clock—sometimes, especially on very warm summer days, it may even be late afternoon, say six o'clock or later. It may be that this is even our second going-out. In any case my mental and spiritual atmosphere is quite different from what it was during our first careless stroll in the morning. The virgin freshness of the early hour has vanished long since. I have worried, and have struggled in the interval with this or that. I have been forced to grit my teeth and overcome one difficulty after the other—I have had a tussle with some person or other. At the same time I have been obliged to keep some diffuse and complicated matter firmly in mind and my head is weary, especially after a successful mastery of the problem. Hence this going a-hunting with Bashan distracts and enlivens me. It infuses me with new life, putting me into condition for the rest of the day and for triumph over the tasks that are still lowering in my path. It is really largely the impulse of gratitude which forces me to describe these hunting trips.

Things, to be sure, are not so neatly

arranged that Bashan and I could go forth
in pursuit of any one special species of the
game which I have mentioned—that we
should, for instance, specialise on rabbits or
ducks. No, on the contrary, we hunt
everything that chances to cross our path—
I had almost said that chances to come
within range of our guns. We need not go
very far in order to strike game. The hunt
may literally begin immediately outside the
garden gate, for there are great numbers
of field-mice and moles in the hollows of
the meadows close behind the house. To
be exact and sportsmanlike—I am aware that
these fur-bearing animals cannot, of course,
be regarded as game in the strict sense of the
term. But their secret, subterranean habits,
especially the nimble craftiness of the mice,
which are not blind o' day like their ex-
cavating and tunnelling brethren, and often
go gambolling upon the surface, and then
when danger approaches go flicking into
the little black burrow without one's being

able to distinguish their legs or their movements—these things work tremendously upon
Bashan's hunting instincts. These are also
the only animals of the wild which occasionally become his prey—a field-mouse, a
mole—these are titbits which are not to be
despised in such lean and meagre days as
these—when one often finds nothing more
palatable than a thick barley soup in the
stoneware bowl beside one's kennel.

I have scarcely taken a dozen steps with
my cane along the poplar avenue, and Bashan
has, as an overture, scarcely got through
with his preliminary leaps and lunges, than
he is seen to be performing the most extraordinary capricoles towards the right. He
is already gripped by the passion for the
chase, and is blind and deaf to all things
save the exciting but hidden goings-on of
the living things about him. With every
nerve taut and tense, waving his tail, carefully lifting his feet, he goes slinking through
the grass, sometimes pausing in mid-step,

with one foreleg and one hindleg in air, then peering with cocked head into the hollows, an action which causes the flaps of his erected ears to fall forward on both sides of his eyes. And then raising both forepaws, he will suddenly jump forward and will stare with dumbfounded expression at a spot where but a moment before there *was* something and where now there is nothing. And then he begins to dig. . . .

I feel a strong desire to go to him and await the result, but then we should never be able to leave the spot. Bashan would expend his entire stock of joy-in-the-chase right here in this meadow, and this stock is meant to last him for the entire day. And so I walk on—untroubled by any thought that he might not be able to overtake me— even though he should remain behind for a long time without having observed in what direction I had gone. To him my track and trail are as clear as that of a bit of game. Should he have lost sight of me, he is sure, with head lowered between his forepaws, to come tearing along this trail. I hear the clinking of his brass license-tag, his firm gallop behind me—and then he goes shooting past me and turns with wagging tail once more to report himself on duty.

Out yonder, however, in the woods or in the broad meadows alongside the brook, I often halt and watch when I catch him digging for a mouse, even though it should be late and I in danger of exceeding the time I have apportioned for my walk. The passionate devotion with which he goes to work is so fascinating to observe, his profound enthusiasm is so contagious, that I cannot but wish him success with all my heart, and naturally I also wish to be a witness of this success. The spot he is attacking may have made quite an innocent impression in its outward aspect—it is, let us say, some mossy little mound at the foot of a birch

and possibly penetrated by its roots.   But
did not my Bashan hear the quarry, scent
it, perhaps even see it as it switched away ?
He is absolutely certain that his bit of game
is sitting there under the earth in some snug
runlet or burrow ; all that is necessary is
to get at it, and so he goes digging away
for all he is worth in absolute devotion to
his task and oblivious to the world.   He
proceeds not ragingly, but with a certain
fine deliberation, with the tempered passion
of the real sportsman—it is wonderful to see.
His small, tiger-striped body beneath the
smooth coat of which the ribs align themselves and the muscles play, is hollowed, is
concave in the middle ; his hindquarters,
with the stump of a tail vibrating to quick
time, is erected vertically.   His head is
between his forepaws and thrust into the
slant hole he has already dug.   With averted
face he continues with the rapid strokes of
his iron claws to tear up the earth more
and more—lumps of sod, pebbles, shreds

of glass, and bits of roots fly all about me. Sometimes his snortings are heard in the silence of the fields—that is when he has succeeded in penetrating some little distance, and in wedging his snout into the entrance to the burrow in order, by means of his scent, to keep check upon the clever, still, and timid creature within there.

His breathing sounds muffled, he ejects his breath in a blast in order to be able to empty his lungs quickly—and to draw in the delicate, acrid, distant, and yet disguised odour of the mice. What emotions must surge through the breast of the little animal down there when it hears this hollow and muffled snorting? Well, that is its own affair, or perhaps God's affair, who has decreed that Bashan shall be the enemy and persecutor of these earth-mice. And then —is not fear only an intensified feeling for life? If no Bashan existed the little mouse would very likely be bored to death. And what use or purpose would then be served

by its beady-eyed cleverness and its art of
swift mining operations, factors that fairly
well equalise the conditions of the battle,
so that the success of the party upon the
offensive always remains highly problem-
atical, even improbable. Indeed I feel no
compassion for the mouse ; inwardly I
take sides with Bashan, and sometimes I
cannot remain content with the rôle of a
mere spectator. I get my walking-stick
into play whenever some firmly-bedded
pebble, some tough cord of a root is in his
way and help him to get rid of these obstacles.
Then sometimes, in the midst of his hot and
furious activity, he will throw up his head
and bestow upon me a swift and fervent
glance of gratitude and approval. With
munching jaws and glinting teeth he goes
working his way into the stubborn, fibrous
ground,—tears away clods, throws them
aside, sends his resonant snorts once more
into the depths, and then, fired to re-
newed action by the provocative scent,

sets his claws once more into furious action. . . .

In the great majority of cases this is all love's labour lost. With the moist earth clinging to his nose and sprinkled about his shoulders, Bashan makes another quick and superficial survey of the territory and then gives it up and jogs indifferently on.

" There was nothing doing, Bashan," I remark to him, when he chances to look at me. " Nothing doing," I repeat, shaking my head and raising my brows and my shoulders, so as to make the message plainer. But it is not at all necessary to comfort him ; his failure does not depress him for a moment. To hunt is to hunt, the titbit of game is the least of all considerations. It was, take it all in all, a magnificent effort he thinks—in so far as he still happens to think of this violent business he has just been through. For now he is already on new adventure bent—adventures of which there is, indeed, no lack in the three zones of this domain.

Sometimes, however, he happens to catch the mouse. And then something occurs which never fails to strike me with horror —for Bashan devours his prey alive, with hide and hair. Perhaps the unfortunate creature had not been properly advised by its instincts of self-preservation and had chosen a spot for its burrow which was too soft, too unprotected and too easily excavated. Perhaps the little creature's tunnels had not been sunk deep enough, or it had been paralysed by fright and prevented from burrowing to deeper levels. Or it had perchance lost its head and, crouching a few inches under the surface with its little beady eyes popping out of their sockets with horror, listened to that terrible snorting coming nearer and nearer. No matter, the iron claws disinter it, uncover it, fling it into the air, into the pitiless glare of the day! Hapless little mouse! you had good cause to be frightened, and it is well that this immense and comprehensible fright has already reduced you to a kind of semi-unconsciousness. For now the tiny rodent is to be converted into pap and pulp.

Bashan has caught it by the tail; he tosses it upon the ground twice or thrice; a very faint squeak is heard, the last that is vouchsafed to the god-forsaken little mouse. And then Bashan snaps it up, and it disappears between his jaws and the white, gleaming teeth. He stands there with legs four square and forepaws braced. His neck is lowered and thrust forth as he chews— he catches at the titbit again and again and throws it into the proper position in his mouth. The tiny bones are heard to crack, a shred of fur hangs for a moment from the corner of his mouth; he draws it in and then all is over. Bashan then executes a kind of dance of joy and triumph, circling around me as I stand leaning on my cane with cold shudders rushing up and down my spine.

' You're a fine fellow ! " I say to him in a kind of gruesome recognition of his victory. " You scoundrel ! you murderer ! you cannibal ! "

These words cause him to dance still more wildly, and, one might say, almost to laugh aloud. So I proceed on my way, somewhat chilled in the limbs owing to the tragedy I have just witnessed, and yet inwardly enlightened by the brutal humour of life. The thing, after all, is quite in order, in Nature's order. A mouselet which had been ill-advised by its faulty instincts has simply been converted into pap and pulp. Nevertheless I am inwardly gratified when in such instances as the foregoing, it did not become necessary for me to help along the natural order of things with my cane, but remained a simple and passive spectator.

Startling and even terrifying is it when some pheasant suddenly bursts from the thicket in which, sleeping or waking, it had hoped to remain undiscovered, some coign of concealment from which Bashan's delicate and unobtrusive nose had after a little searching managed to rouse it.   Thumping and flapping, with frightened and indignant cries and cacklings, the large, rust-red and long-tailed bird lifts itself a-wing, and with all the silly heedlessness of a hen, goes scattering upon some tree from which it begins to scold, whilst Bashan, erect against the trunk, barks up at the fowl, stormily, savagely. The meaning behind this barking is clear. It says plainly enough: " Get off ! get off that perch ! Tend to business. Fly off, so I can have my bit o' fun. Get off—I want to chase you ! "   The pheasant cannot, apparently, resist this powerful voice, and off it scuds, making its way with heavy flight through the branches, still cackling and complaining, whilst Bashan, full of manly silence, pursues it smartly along the level ground.

This is sufficient for Bashan's bliss; his

wish and his will go no farther. What would have happened had he caught the bird? Nothing, I assure you, absolutely nothing. I once saw him with a bird between his claws. He had probably come upon it whilst it lay in deep sleep, so that the clumsy thing had had no time to lift itself from the ground. On that occasion Bashan had stood over the fowl, an utterly bewildered victor, and did not know what to do next. With one wing raked wide open and with its head drawn aside to the very limit of its neck, the pheasant lay in the grass and screamed, screamed without a single pause —a passer-by might have thought that some old woman was being murdered in the bushes. I hurried up, bent upon preventing something horrible. But I was soon convinced that there was nothing to fear. Bashan's all-too conspicuous confusion, the half-curious, half-disgusted mien with which, head aslant, he looked down upon his prisoner, assured me of that. This old wives' screeching and dinning in his ears, very likely got upon his nerves—the whole affair apparently caused him more embarrassment than triumph. Was it in victory or in shame that he pulled a couple of feathers out of his victim's dress, very, very cautiously with his mouth, refraining from all use of his teeth, and then threw them aside with an angry toss of his head ?

He followed this tribute to his predatory instincts by taking his paw off his victim and letting it go free—not out of magnanimity, to be sure, but simply because the situation bored him, and because it really had nothing in common with the stir and gaiety of the chase. Never had I seen a more astonished bird ! It had closed its account with life, and for a brief space it seemed that it no longer knew what use to make of life, for it lay in the grass as though dead. It then tottered along the ground for a bit, swung clumsily upon a tree,

appeared about to fall from it, summoned
its strength, and then with heavily-dragging
feathery raiment went fluttering off into
the distance. It no longer squawked, but
kept its bill shut. Silently the bird flew
across the park, the river, the forest beyond
the river, away, away, as far as its short
wings could carry it. It is certain that this
particular pheasant never returned to this
particular spot.

There are, however, a good many of his
breed in our hunting-grounds, and Bashan
hounds and hunts them in an honourable
sportsmanlike manner and according to the
rules of the game. The only real blood-guilt
that lies heavy upon his head is the devouring
of the field-mice, and this, too, appears as
something incidental and negligible. It is
the scenting-out, the drive, the pursuit,
which serve him as a noble end in themselves—all who were able to observe him at
this brilliant game would come to the same
conclusion. How beautiful he grows, how

ideal, how perfect to the end and purpose ! It is thus that the awkward and loutish peasant lad of the hills becomes perfect and picturesque when you see him standing amidst the rocks and cliffs as a hunter of the *Gemsbock*. All that is noble, genuine, and fine in Bashan is driven to the surface and achieves a glorious efflorescence in such hours as these. That is why he pants for these hours with such intensity and why he suffers so poignantly when they pass unused.

Bashan is no toy spaniel ; he is the veritable woodsman and pathfinder, such as figure heroically in books. A great joy in himself, in his own existence cries from every one of the martial, masculine, and striking poses which he assumes and which succeed one another with almost cinematographic rapidity. There are few things which are able so to refresh my eyes as the sight of him, as he goes sailing through the underbrush in a light, feathering trot and

then suddenly stands at gaze, with one paw
daintily raised and bent inward, sagacious,
vigilant, impressive, with all his faculties in
a radiant intensification. And then amidst
all this imposing statuesqueness it is possible
that he may give vent to a sudden squeak,
or yelp, occasioned, very likely, by having
caught his foot in something thorny. But
this too, is all in order with the course of
nature and with the perfection of the picture
—this cheery readiness to be splendidly
simple. It is capable of diminishing his
dignity only as a breath dims a mirror;
the superbness of his carriage is restored
the very next moment.

I look upon him—my Bashan—and I am
reminded of a time during which he lost
all his pride and his gallant poise, and was
once more reduced to that condition of
bodily and mental dejection in which we
first saw him in the kitchen of that tavern
in the mountains, and from which he so
painfully lifted himself to a faith in his

own personality and in life. I do not know
what ailed him—he began to bleed from the
mouth or the nose or the ears—even to-day
I have no clear idea of his particular malady.
But wherever he went in those days, he left
marks of blood behind him—in the grass
of the hunting-grounds, in the straw of his
kennel, on the floor of the house when he
entered it—and yet there was no external
injury anywhere visible. At times his entire
nose seemed to be covered with red paint.
Whenever he sneezed he would send forth
a spray of blood, and then he would step
in the drops and leave brick-red impressions
of his paws wherever he went. Careful
examinations were made, but these led to
no results and thus brought about increased
anxieties. Were his lungs attacked? or
was he afflicted by some mysterious dis-
temper of which we had never heard?—
something to which his breed was subject?
Since the strange as well as unpleasant
phenomena did not cease after some days, it

was decided that he must go to the Dog's Hospital.

Kindly but firmly Bashan's master imposed upon him on the day following—it was about noon—the leathern muzzle—that mask of stubborn meshes which Bashan loathes above all things and of which he always seeks to rid himself by violent shakings of his head and furious rubbings of his paws. He was fastened to the braided leash and thus harnessed was led up the avenue—on the left-hand side—then through the local park and a suburban street into the group of buildings belonging to the High School. We passed beneath the portal and crossed the courtyard. We then entered a waiting-room, against the walls of which sat a number of persons all of whom, like myself, held a dog on a leash—dogs of different breeds and sizes, who regarded one another with melancholy eyes through their leather muzzles. There was an old and motherly dame with her fat and apoplectic pug, a

footman in livery with a tall and snow-white
Russian deerhound, who emitted from time
to time a dry and aristocratic cough ; a
countryman with a *dachshund*—apparently
a case for orthopedic science, since all his
feet were planted upon his body in the most
crooked and distorted manner, and many
others. The attendant at this veterinary
clinic admitted the patients one after the
other into the adjoining consulting-room.
At length the door to this was also opened
for me and Bashan.

The Professor was a man of advanced
age, and was clad in a long, white oper-
ating coat. He wore gold-rimmed spec-
tacles, his head was crowned with gray
curls and his whole manner was so amiable
and conveyed such an air of wise kindli-
ness that I would immediately have en-
trusted myself and my family to him in
any emergency. Whilst I gave him my
account of things, he smiled paternally
upon his patient, who sat there in front

of him and turned up to him a pair of humble and trustful eyes.

" He's got fine eyes," said the doctor, without allowing Bashan's hybrid goatee to disturb him, and declared that he was ready to make an investigation at once. Bashan, quite helpless with astonishment, was now, with the aid of the attendant, spread upon the table. It was moving to see how the old doctor applied the stethoscope to the breast of the tiger-striped little manikin and performed his auscultation, just as I had seen it done in my case more than once. He listened to the swift workings of the tiny canine heart, and sounded his entire organic internal functions from different points of his exterior. Hereupon, tucking his stethoscope under his arm, he began to examine Bashan's eyes with both hands, his nose as well as the roof of his mouth, and then ventured upon delivering a preliminary prognosis.

The dog, said he, was a trifle nervous and

anæmic, but otherwise in good condition.
It might be epitaksis or hæmathemesis. But
it might also be a case of tracheal or pharyn-
geal hemorrhage—this was by no means
precluded. For the present one would be
most inclined to call it a case of hæmoptysis.
It was necessary to keep the animal under
careful observation. I should do best to
leave him here and then call and inquire
again in the course of a week.

Thus instructed, I expressed my thanks
and gave Bashan a farewell pat on the
shoulder. I saw how the attendant led
Bashan across the courtyard towards the
entrance to a building at the rear, and how
Bashan, with a bewildered and anxious expression on his face, looked back at me.
And yet he should have felt flattered, just as
I could not help feeling flattered by hearing
the Professor declare him to be nervous
and anæmic. No one who had stood at his
cradle would ever have imagined that it was
written in his horoscope that he was one

day to be said to be suffering from two such fashionable ailments, or that Medical Science would be called in to deliberate over him with such gravity and solicitude.

From that day on my walks were to me what unsalted food is to the palate—they gave me little pleasure. No silent tumult of joy burst upon me when I went out— under way no proud, high, mad helter-skelter of the chase surrounded me. The park seemed to me desolate—I was bored. I did not fail to make inquiries by telephone during the interval of waiting. The answer, communicated from some subordinate quarter, was to the effect that the health of the patient was as good as could be expected under the circumstances—circumstances which, for good reasons or for bad, one did not trouble to designate more clearly. As soon as the day arrived on which I had taken Bashan to the veterinary institution, and the week was up, I once more made my way to the place.

Guided by numerous signboards with inscriptions and pointing hands, liberally affixed to walls and doors, I managed, without going astray, to negotiate the door of the clinical department which sheltered Bashan. In accordance with the command upon an enamelled plate on the door, I forbore to knock, and walked in. The rather large room in which I found myself gave me the impression of a wild-beast house in a menagerie. The atmosphere incidental to such a house also prevailed here, with the exception that the odour of the menagerie seemed to be mingled here with all kinds of sweetish medicinal vapours—a cloying and rather disturbing mixture. Cages with bars were set all around the walls, and nearly all of them were occupied. Resolute barks saluted me from one of these. A man, evidently the keeper, was busy with a rake and a shovel before the open door of one of these cages. He was pleased to respond to my greeting without interrupting his work, and then left me for the present entirely to my own impressions.

My first survey of the scene, whilst the door was still open, had at once revealed to me the whereabouts of Bashan, and so I went up to him. He lay behind the bars of his cage upon some loose stuff which must have been made of tan-bark or something similar, and which added its own peculiar aroma to the odour of the animals and of the carbolic acid or lysoform. He lay there like a leopard, though a very weary, very disinterested and disappointed leopard. I was shocked by the sullen indifference with which he greeted my entrance and advance. He merely gave a feeble thump or two upon the floor of his cage with his tail, and only after I had spoken to him did he deign to raise his head from his paws, but only to drop it again almost immediately and to blink moodily to one side. A stoneware vessel full of water stood at the back of his cage. Outside, attached to the bars of his cage, there was a small wooden frame with a card, partly-printed, partly hand-written, which contained an account of Bashan's name, breed, sex, and age. Beneath this there was a fever-index curve.

" Bastard setter," I read. Name : Bashan. Male. Two years old. Brought in on such and such a day and month of the year —to be observed for occult hemorrhages. And then followed the curve of Bashan's temperature, drawn in ink and showing no great variations. There were also details in figures regarding the frequency of Bashan's pulse. So his temperature was being taken and even his pulse counted—nothing was lacking in this respect. It was his frame of mind which occasioned me worry.

" Is that one yourn ? " asked the attendant who, implements in hand, had in the meantime approached me. He was a stocky, round-bearded and red-cheeked man, wearing a kind of gardener's apron, with brown, somewhat bloodshot eyes, the moist and honest glances of which had something astonishingly dog-like in them.

I answered his question in the affirmative, referred to the order I had received to call again to-day, to the telephone conversations I had carried on, and declared that I had come to see how everything stood. The man cast a glance at the card. Yes, he said, the dog was suffering from occult hemorrhages, and that kind of thing always took a long time—especially if one didn't know where the hemorrhages came from. Well, wasn't that always the case? No, one didn't know anything about it as yet. But the dog was there to be observed and he was being observed. The hemorrhages were still occurring, were they? Yes, they came on now and then. And they were being observed? Yes, most carefully.

" Has he any fever ? " I asked, trying to make something out of the chart hanging on the bars. No, no fever. The dog had

quite a normal temperature and pulse, about
ninety beats in the minute—that was the
normal number, that was about right, they
ought not to be less, but if they were fewer,
then he would have to be observed still more
sharply. The dog—if it wasn't for these
here occult hemorrhages, was really in pretty
good condition. Of course he had howled
at first, a full twenty-four hours, but after
that he had got used to things. Of course,
he didn't eat much, but then he got very
little exercise, and it was also a question of
how much he was accustomed to eat. What
food did they give him? Soup, said the
man. But as he had already remarked, the
dog didn't eat much of it.

"He has a very depressed look," I said,
affecting an expert air. Yes, no doubt of
that, said the man, but then that didn't
really mean much. For it wasn't very nice
for a dog to have to be cooped up in that
way and be observed. They were all
depressed more or less, that is to say, the

good-natured ones, but there were some as got mean and nasty. But he couldn't say as this here dog had. This dog of mine was a good-natured sort and wouldn't think of biting—even though one were to observe him till Doomsday. I agreed with what the man said, though indignation and anxiety gnawed at my heart. How long, I asked him, did one think it was necessary to keep Bashan here? The man cast another glance at the chart. Another week, he remarked, would be necessary to observe him properly —that's what the Professor had said. I might come after another week and inquire again—that would make two weeks in all, and then I would be able to get exact information about the dog and about curing his occult hemorrhages.

I went—after I had made another attempt to cheer up Bashan's spirits by talking to him. But he was as little affected by my going away as by my coming. He seemed to be oppressed by a feeling of dark hopelessness—and contempt. "Since you have been capable," his attitude seemed to declare, "of having me put into this cage, I expect nothing more from you." And was it not in truth enough to make him despair of all reason and justice? What had he done that this should happen to him? How came it that I not only permitted it, but even took the initial steps? I had meant to act well by him. He had begun to bleed from the nose, and though this did not appear to disturb him in any way, I had nevertheless thought it fitting that veterinary science should be consulted, as befitted a dog in good circumstances, and I had also learned that he was rather anæmic and nervous— like the daughter of an earl. How could I know that such a fate awaited him? How could I make him understand that he was having honours and attention bestowed upon him by being locked behind bars—like a jaguar—in being deprived of air, sunshine, and exercise, and instead of being able to enjoy these blessings, tormented with a thermometer day after day?

Such were the questions which I put to myself as I walked home. Whilst I had up to then only missed Bashan, I now began to be afflicted with a positive anxiety for him, for the welfare of his soul, and was forced to contend with doubt and self-accusatory thoughts. After all, was it not mere vanity and egoistic conceit which had induced me to take him to this canine infirmary? Besides, was it not possible, that a secret wish had been the wellspring of this action, a wish to get rid of him for a time, a certain ignoble curiosity to free myself from his incessant watching, and to see how it would feel to be able to turn calmly to the right or to the left without bringing about emotional cataclysms in the animated world without—emotional tempests whether of joy or sorrow, or bitter disillusionment? It was not to be denied—since Bashan's internment I was enjoying a definite feeling

of independence such as I had not known
for a long time. When I glanced through the
glass door of my study there was no one
there to annoy me with the spectacle of his
martyrdom of patience. No one came with
paw hesitatingly raised, so that, giving way
to a burst of pitying laughter, I should be
forced to deny my own fixed resolution and
go forth earlier than I had intended. No
one questioned my right to go into the
house or into the park, just as the spirit
moved me. This was a comfortable condition of things, quieting and full of the charm
of novelty. But as the accustomed incentive
was lacking, I almost ceased to go walking
at all. My health suffered in consequence,
and whilst my condition grew to be re-
markably like that of Bashan in his
cage, I indulged in the moral reflection
that the fetters of sympathy would have
been more conducive to my own comfort
than the egoistic freedom for which I had
panted.

The second week elapsed in good time, and so, on the day appointed, I and the bearded attendant stood once more in front of Bashan's barred habitation. The inmate lay upon his side, stretched out in a posture of absolute indifference upon the tan-bark of his cage, bits of which flecked his coat. He was staring backward at the chalky wall of his prison with eyes that were glassy and dull. He did not move. His breathing was scarcely perceptible. Only, from time to time, his chest—which displayed every rib—rose in a sob which he breathed forth with a soft and heartrending tremolo of his vocal chords. His legs seemed to have grown too long, his paws huge and unshapely—due to his terrible emaciation. His coat was extremely rough and dishevelled and crushed, and, as already remarked, soiled from wallowing in the tan-bark. He paid no attention to me, and it seemed that he would never again be able to summon up enough energy to take an interest in anything.

The hemorrhages, said the attendant, had not quite disappeared—they still happened now and then. Their origin was not as yet quite clear, but in any case they were of a harmless nature. I was free to leave the dog there for a still longer period of observation—in order to make quite sure— or I might take him home with me, where he would no doubt get rid of the evil—all in good time. I then drew out the plaited leather leash from my pocket and said that I would take Bashan with me. The attendant thought that would be very sensible. He opened the barred door and we both called Bashan by name, alternately and both together—but he did not stir. He merely kept staring at the whitewashed wall opposite. He made no resistance when I thrust my arm into the cage and pulled him out by the collar. He gave a kind of convulsive flounce about and landed on his legs on the floor. There he stood with his tail between his legs, his ears retracted, a very picture of misery.

I picked him up, gave the attendant a tip, and left the ward of this canine hospital. I then proceeded to pay my bill in the office of the institution. This bill, at seventy-five pfennigs a day and the veterinary's fee for the first examination, amounted to twelve marks, fifty pfennigs. I then led Bashan home, clothed in the stern yet sweetish atmosphere of the clinic which still permeated my companion's coat.

He was broken in body and in soul. Animals are more unrestrained and primitive, less subject to inhibitions of all kinds, and therefore in a certain sense more human in the physical expression of their moods than we. Forms and figures of speech which survive among us only in a kind of mental or moral translation, or as metaphors, are still true and valid when applied to them. They live up to the expression in the fullest, freshest sense of the term—and in this there

is something wonderfully enlivening to the
eye. Bashan, as one would say, " let his
head hang," or " had a hang-dog look."
He did actually hang his head—hung it low
ike some wrack of a wornout cab-horse
which, with abscesses on its legs and period-
ical shivers undulant along its sides, stands
at its post with a hundredweight of woe
pulling its poor nose, swarming with flies,
towards the pavement.

These two weeks, at the veterinary high
school, as I have already said, had reduced
him to the very condition in which I had
first found him in the foot-hills. Perhaps
I ought to say that he was only the shadow
of himself—if this would not be an insult
to the proud and joyous Bashan. The smell
of the dog-hospital which he had brought
with him, vanished in the washtrays, after
several ablutions with soap and hot water—
vanished—all save a few floating and rebel-
lious whiffs. A bath may be said to exercise
a spiritual influence, may be said to possess

a symbolic significance to us human beings—
but no one would dare to say that the physica
cleansing of poor Bashan, meant the restora-
tion of his customary spirits. I took him to
the hunting-grounds on the very first day
of his home-coming. But he went slinking
at my heels with silly look and lolling
tongue, and the pheasants were jubilant
over a close season. At home he would
remain lying for days as I had last seen him
stretched out in his cage at the hospital,
and staring with glassy eyes, inwardly limp
and without a trace of his wholesome impatience, without making a single attempt
to force me to go forth for a walk. On the
contrary I was forced to fetch him from
his berth at the tiny door of his kennel
and to spur him on and up. Even the
wild and indiscriminate way in which he
wolfed his food, reminded me of his sordid
youth.

And then it was a great joy to see how
he found himself again, how his greeting

gradually took on the old, warm-hearted, playful impetuosity, how, instead of coming towards me with a sullen limp, he would once more come storming upon me in swift response to my morning whistle, so that he might put his forepaws on my chest and snap at my face. It was wonderful to see how the joy in his mere body and in his senses returned to him in the wide spaces and the open air—and to observe those daring and picturesque positions he would assume, those swift plunging pounces with drawn-up feet which he would make upon some tiny creature in the high grass—all these things came back and refreshed my eyes. Bashan began to forget. That hateful incident of his internment, an incident so absolutely senseless from Bashan's point of view, sank into oblivion, unredeemed, to be sure, unexplained by any clear understanding —something which, after all, would have been impossible. But time swallowed it up and enveloped it, even as time must heal these things where human beings are concerned, and so we went on with our lives as before, whilst the inexpressible thing sank deeper and deeper into forgetfulness. For some weeks longer it happened that Bashan would occasionally sport an incarnadined nose, then the phenomenon vanished, and became a thing of the past. And so, after all, it mattered little whether it had been a case of epistaksis or of hæmathemesis. . . .

There—I have told the story of the clinic —against my own better resolution. May the reader forgive this lengthy digression and return with me to the chase in the hunting-grounds which we had interrupted. Ah, have you ever heard that tearful yowling with which a dog, mustering his utmost forces, takes up the pursuit of a rabbit in flight—that yowling in which fury and bliss, longing and ecstatic despair mix and mingle? How often have I heard Bashan give vent to this ! It is a grand passion, desired, sought for and deliriously enjoyed which goes ringing through the landscape, and every time this wild cry comes to my ear from near or far, I am given a shock of pleasant fright, and the thrill goes tingling through all my limbs. Then I hurry forwards, or to the left or right, rejoicing that Bashan is to get his money's worth to-day, and I strive mightily to bring the chase within my range of vision. And when this chase goes storming past me in full and furious career, I stand banned and tense, even though the negative outcome of the venture is certain from the beginning, and I look on whilst an excited smile draws taut the muscles of my face.

And what of the rabbit—the timid, the tricky? He switches his ears through the air, crocks his head backwards at an angle, and runs for dear life in long, lunging leaps, throwing his whitish-yellow scut into the air. Thus he goes scratching and scudding in front of Bashan, who is howling inwardly. And yet the rabbit in the depths of his fearsome and flighty soul ought to know that he is in no serious danger and that he will manage to escape, just as his brothers and sisters and he himself have always managed to escape. Not once in all his life has Bashan managed to catch a single rabbit, and it is practically beyond the bounds of possibility that he ever should. Many dogs, as the old proverb goes, bring about the death of the rabbit—a clear proof that a single dog cannot manage it. For the rabbit is a master of the quick and sudden turn-about—a feat quite beyond the capacity of Bashan, and it is this feat which decides the whole matter. It is an infallible weapon and an attribute of the animal that is born to fight with flight—a means of escape which can be applied at any moment and which it carries in its instincts in order to put it into use at precisely that moment when victory is almost within Bashan's grasp. And alas, Bashan is then betrayed and sold.

Here they come shooting diagonally
through the woods, flash across the path on
which I am standing, and then go dashing
towards the river, the rabbit dumb and
bearing his inherited trick in his heart,
Bashan yammering in high and heady tones.
" No howling now ! " I say or think to
myself. " You are wasting strength, strength
of lung, strength of breath, which you ought
to be saving up and concentrating—so that
you can grab him ! " I am forced to think
thus, because I am on Bashan's side, because
his passion is infectious—imperatives which
force me to hope fervently that he will
succeed—even at the peril of seeing him
tear the rabbit to pieces before my eyes.
Ah, how he runs ! How beautiful it is,
how edifying to see a living creature un-
folding all its forces in some supreme effort.
My dog runs better than this rabbit ; his
muscular system is stronger ; the distance
between them has visibly diminished—ere
they are lost to sight. I leave the path and

hurry through the park towards the left, going in the direction of the river-bank. I emerge upon the gravelly street just in time to see the mad chase come ravening on from the right—the hopeful, infinitely thrilling chase—for Bashan is almost at the heels of the rabbit. He is silent now; he is running with his teeth set, the close proximity of the scent urges him to the final effort.

" One last plunge, Bashan," I think, and would like to shout to him—" just one more—aim well ! keep cool ! And beware of the turnabout ! " But these thoughts have scarcely flashed through my brain than the " turnabout," the " hook," the *volte-face*, has taken place—the catastrophe is upon us. My gallant dog makes the decisive forward plunge—but . . . at the selfsame moment there is a short jerk, and with pert and limber swiftness the rabbit switches aside at a right angle to the course—and Bashan goes shooting past the hindquarters of his quarry

—shooting straight ahead, howling, desperate
and with all his feet stemmed as brakes—so
that the dust and gravel go flying. By the
time he has overcome his momentum, flung
himself right about and gained leeway in
the new direction—whilst, I say, he has
done this in agony of soul and with wailings
of woe, the rabbit has won a considerable
handicap towards the woods—yes, he is
even lost to the eyes of his pursuer, for
during the convulsive application of his four
brakes, the pursuer could not see whither
the pursued had turned.

" It's no use," I think, " it may be
beautiful, but it is surely futile." The wild
pursuit vanishes in the distances of the park
and in the opposite direction.   " There
ought to be more dogs—five or six—a whole
pack of dogs ! There ought to be dogs to
cut him off on the flank, dogs to cut him off
ahead, dogs to drive him into a corner, dogs
to be in at the death."   And in my mind's
eye, in my excitement, I behold a whole

pack of fox-hounds with lolling tongues go storming upon the rabbit in their midst.

I think these things and dream these dreams out of a sheer passion for the chase, for what has the rabbit done to me that I should wish him to meet with so terrible an end? It is true that Bashan is closer to me than the long-eared one, and it is quite in order that I should share his feelings and accompany him with my good wishes for his success. But then the rabbit is also a warm, furry, breathing bit of our common life. He has played his trick upon my hunting dog not out of malice, but out of the urgent wish to be able to nibble soft tree-shoots a little longer and to bring forth young.

Nevertheless my thoughts continue to weave themselves about the matter and about. As, for example: " It would, of course, be quite another matter, if this"—and I lift and regard the walking-stick in my hand—" if this cane here were not so useless and benign an instrument, but a thing of more serious construction and constitution, pregnant with lightning and operative at a distance, by means of which I could come to the assistance of the gallant Bashan and hold up the rabbit, so that he would remain flop upon the spot—after doing a fine *salto mortale*. Then there would be no need of other hounds, and Bashan would have done his duty if he had merely brought me the rabbit."

The way things shape themselves, however, it is Bashan who sometimes goes tumbling head over heels when he tries to meet and counter that damnable quick turn, and sometimes it is also the rabbit who does the somersault, though this is a mere trifle to the latter, something quite in order and inconsequential and certainly by no means identified with any feeling of abject misery. For Bashan, however, it means a severe concussion, which might some time or other lead to his breaking his neck.

Often a rabbit-chase comes to an end in a few minutes, that is to say, when the rabbit succeeds after a few hot lengths of running, in ducking into the underbrush and hiding, or in throwing his pursuer off his trail by means of feints and quick double turns, so that the four-legged hunter, sorely puzzled and uncertain, jumps hither and thither, whilst I shout bloodthirsty advice to him and with frantic gesticulations of my cane try to point out to him the direction in which I saw the rabbit escape.

Sometimes the hunt extends itself throughout the length and breadth of the landscape, so that Bashan's voice, wildly yowling, sounds like a hunting-horn ringing through the region from afar, now nearer and now farther away, whilst I, awaiting his return, calmly go my ways. And, great Heavens! in what a condition he *does* return! Foam drips from his jaws, his thighs are lax and hollow, his ribs flutter, his tongue hangs long and loose from his maw, inordinately

gaping, something which causes his drunken
and swimming eyes to appear distorted and
slant, Mongolian, the while his breathing
goes like a steam-engine.

" Lie down, Bashan ! " I command him,
" take a rest, or you'll have apoplexy of the
lungs ! " I halt so as to give him time to
recover. In winter when there is a cold
frost and I see him pumping the icy air with
hoarse pantings into his overheated interior
and then puffing it forth in the form of
white steam, or else swallowing whole hand-
fuls of snow in order to cool his thirst, I
grow quite terrified. Nevertheless, whilst
he lies there, gazing up at me with confused
eye, now and again snapping up his drib-
blings, I cannot refrain from poking a bit
of fun at him, because of the unalterable
futility of his efforts.

" Bashan ! where's that rabbit ! Aren't
you going to fetch me that rabbit ! " Then
he begins to thump the ground with his tail,
and interrupts for a moment whilst I am

speaking the spasmodic pumping machinery of his sides. He snaps in embarrassment, for he does not know that my ridicule is intended merely to conceal from him and from myself an accretion of shame and guilty conscience, because I, on my part, was not man enough to " hold up " the rabbit—as is the duty of a real master. He is unaware of all this, and so it is easy for me to make fun and to put the matter as though *he* were in some way to blame. . . .

Strange things sometimes occur during these hunts. I shall never forget how the rabbit once ran into my very arms. It happened along the river, or rather upon the small and clayey bank above it. Bashan was in full cry after his quarry and I was approaching the zone of the river-bank from the direction of the wood. I broke through the thistle stalks along the gravel slope and sprang down the grass-covered declivity on to the path at the very moment that the rabbit, with Bashan some fifteen paces behind him,

was coming towards me in long bounds
from the direction of the ferryman's house,
towards which I was turning. Bunny came
running along the middle of the path straight
towards me. . . .

My first, hunter-like and hostile impulse
was to take advantage of the situation and to
bar his way, driving him, if possible, back
into the jaws of his pursuer, who came on
yelping in poignant joy. There I stood, as
though rooted to the spot, and, slave that I
was to the fever of the chase, I simply
balanced the stick in my hand whilst the
rabbit came nearer and nearer. I knew
that a rabbit's vision is very poor, that alone
the sense of hearing and the sense of smell
are able to convey warnings to him. He
might therefore possibly mistake me for a
tree as I stood there—it was my plan and
my lively desire that he should do this, and so
succumb to a fatal error, the consequences
of which were not quite clear to me, but of
which I nevertheless thought to make use.

Whether the rabbit really made such an error during the course of his advance, is not quite clear. . . . I believe that he noticed me only at the very last moment, for what he did was so unexpected that all my schemes and deliberations were at once reduced to nothing, and a deep, sudden, and startling change took place in my state of mind.

Was the little animal beside itself with mortal fear ? Enough, it leaped upon me, just like a little dog, ran up my overcoat with its tiny paws, and, still upright, struggled to bore itself into the depths of my chest—the terrible chest of the master of the chase. With upraised arms and my body bent backwards, I stood there and looked down upon the rabbit who, on his part, looked up at me. We stood thus for only a second, perhaps it was only the fraction of a second, but thus and there we stood. I saw him with such strange, disconcerting minuteness, saw his long ears, of which one stood upright, whilst the other hung down, saw his great, clear, protuberant, short-sighted eyes, his rough lip, and the long hairs of his whiskers, the white on his breast and the little paws. I felt, or seemed to feel the pounding of his harried little heart. It was very strange to see him thus plainly and to have him so close to me, the little familiar spirit of the place, the secret throbbing heart of the landscape, this ever evasive creature which I had seen only for a few brief moments in its meadows and downs as it went scudding comically away. And now in the extremity of its need and helplessness it was nestling up against me and clutching my coat, clutching at the breast of a man—not the man, it seemed to me, who was Bashan's master, but the breast of one who is also the master of the rabbit and of Bashan and of Bashan's master. This lasted, as I have said, only a brief moment or so, and then the rabbit had dropped off, had once more taken to his unequal legs and jumped down the escarpment to the left, whilst Bashan had now arrived in his place—Bashan with horrible hue-and-cry and with all the heady tones of his frenetic hunting-howls—all of which suffered swift interruption on his arrival. For a well-aimed blow of the stick delivered with malice prepense by the master of the rabbit, sent him yelping with smarting hindquarters down the slope to the right, up which he was forced to climb—with a limp—before he was once more able, after considerable delay, to take up the trail of the no longer visible quarry.

And then finally there is the hunt after water-fowl to which I must also dedicate a few lines. This hunt can take place only during winter and the colder part of the spring, before the birds migrate from their quarters near the city to the lakes—the suburbs here serving them merely as a kind of emergency halting-place in obedience to the demands of the stomach. This hunt is less exciting than the rabbit hunt is likely to be, but like this it has something that is attractive both to hunter and to hound, or rather to the hunter and his master. The master is captivated by these forays after the wild fowl chiefly in consideration of the landscape, since the friendly nearness of the water is connected with them, but also because it diverts and edifies him to study the form of life practised by these swimmers and flyers, thus emerging a little out of his own rut and experimenting with theirs.

The attitude towards life assumed by the ducks is more amiable, more bourgeois, and more comfortable than that of the gulls. Nearly always they appear to be full and contented, little troubled by the cares of subsistence—no doubt because they always chance to find what they seek, and because the table, so to speak, is always set for them. For, as I observe, they eat nearly everything— worms, snails, insects, or even green ooze from the water, and enjoy vast stretches of leisure which enable them to sit and sun themselves on the stones, with bills tucked comfortably under one wing for a little siesta or preening and oiling their plumage so that it does not come into contact with the water at all, but rather causes this to pearl off from the surface in a string of nervous drops. Or you may catch them going for a mere pleasure ride or swim upon the racing stream, lifting their pointed tails into the air, and turning and twisting and shrugging their shoulders in bland self-satisfaction.

But in the nature of the gulls there is something wild and hectic, dreary and sad and monotonous ; they are invested with an air of desperate and hungry depredation. Almost all day long they go crying around the waterfall in bevies and in slant transverse flight, or curving about the place where the brownish waters pour from the mouths of the great pipes into the stream. For the

swift, darting plunge for fish which some of
these gulls practise is scarcely sufficiently
rich in results to still their raw and ranging
mass-hunger, and the titbits with which
they are frequently forced to content themselves as they swoop above the overflows
and carry away mysterious fragments in
their bent beaks, must sometimes be far from
appetising. They do not like the banks of
the river. But when the water is low they
stand and huddle in close crowds upon the
rocks, which are then free of water, and
these they cover with their white feathery
masses—just as the crags and islets of the
northern seas squirm and writhe with untold
numbers of nesting eider-ducks.

When Bashan, barking from the shore
across the intervening flood, threatens their
security, then it is a fine sight to see them
all rise simultaneously into the air with loud
cries and caws. But there is no need of
their feeling themselves menaced ; there
is no real danger. For quite apart from

his inborn aversion to water, Bashan harbours
a very wise and entirely justifiable fear of
the current of the river. He knows that his
strength could not possibly cope with this
and that it would infallibly bear him off,
God knows whither or to what distances,
presumably as far as the Danube, where he
would arrive, however, in an extremely
disfigured condition. This is a contingency
of which we have already had ocular evidence
in the shape of bloated cadavers of cats
which were en route to those far-off parts.
He will never venture into the river farther
than the first submerged stones that line
the bank—even though the fierce and ecstatic
lust of the chase should be tugging at his
limbs—even though he should wear a mien
as though he were about to plunge himself
into the waves—yes, the very next moment !
Full confidence, however, may be placed in
his caution, which remains active and vigilant
beneath all this external show of passionate
abandon. There is a distinct purpose behind

all these mimetic onsets, these spectacular preparations for action—they are empty threats which in the last analysis are not really dictated by passion at all, but are calculated with the utmost *sangfroid* merely to intimidate the webfooted foe.

But the gulls, true to their names, are far too poorly equipped in head and heart to be capable of mocking his efforts. Bashan cannot get at them, but he can send his barks against them, send his voice thundering across the water. This voice has the effect of something material—an onset which flutters them and cows them and which they are unable to resist for long. True, they make the attempt to do so ; they remain seated, but an uneasy movement goes through the writhing mass. They turn their heads, ever and anon one of them will lift its wings upon a chance, until suddenly the whole crew, like a whitish cloud, from the core of which come bitter and fatalistic caws, goes rustling and rushing up into the air—

with Bashan jumping about hither and
thither on the stones in order to scare and
scatter them and keep them in motion. For
that is the thing to do—to keep them in
motion—they must not be permitted to rest ;
they must fly up-stream and down-stream,
so that he may chase them.

Bashan goes scouring along the banks,
nosing along their entire length, for everywhere there are ducks at rest, with bills
tucked cunningly and comfortably under
their wings, and wherever he chances to go
they fly up in front of his nose, so that his
progress is like a gay sweeping-clean and
whirling up of the entire strip of sand. They
glide and plump into the water which buoys
and turns them about in security, or they
go flying over his head with bills and necks
outstretched, whilst Bashan, running along
the bank, measures the power of his legs
with that of their pinions.

He is ravished and grateful if they will
but fly, if they will only deign to give

him an opportunity for a bit of glorious
coursing up and down the river. They are
no doubt aware of these wishes of his, and
are even capable of utilising them for their
own benefit. I saw a mother duck with her
brood—it was in the spring, and the river
was already void of birds—this one alone
had remained behind with her young who
were not yet able to fly, and she was guarding
them in a slime-covered puddle which had
been left by the last flood-water and which
filled a depression in the dry bed of the
stream. It was there that Bashan chanced
upon them—I observed the scene from the
upper way. He sprang into the puddle,
sprang into it with barkings and savage
truculent motions, and scattered the family
of ducks in a most deplorable fashion. To
be sure, he did no harm to any member of
this family, but he frightened them all
beyond expression, and the ducklings, flapping their stumps of wings, plunged wildly
in all directions.

The mother duck, however, was seized by that maternal heroism which will hurl itself blindly and full of mad courage even against the most formidable foe in order to protect the brood, and which frequently knows how to bewilder and fluster this foe by a delirious courage which apparently exceeds the limits of nature. With every feather ruffled and with bill horribly agape, the bird fluttered repeatedly against Bashan's face in attack after attack, making one heroic offensive after another against him, hissing portentously the while. And actually her wild and uncompromising aspect brought about a confused retreat on the part of the enemy, without, however, inducing him to quit the field of battle for good, for with a great hullabaloo and clamour he still persisted in advancing anew. The duck-mother thereupon changed her tactics and chose the part of wisdom since heroism had shown itself to be impracticable. It is more than likely that she knew Bashan from some previous experience, was fully acquainted with his weaknesses and childish desires. So she abandoned her little ones—that is, she *apparently* abandoned them. She took refuge in cunning, flew up, flew across the river, " pursued " by Bashan—pursued, as was his firm belief—whilst in reality it was she who led him, led him by the fool's tether of his dominant passion. She flew with the stream, then against it, farther and farther, whilst Bashan raced beside her, so far down-stream and away from the puddle with the ducklings that I lost sight of both the duck and the dog as I walked on. Later on my good dolt came back to me, quite winded and panting furiously. But when we again passed that puddle, it was empty of its erstwhile tenants.

Such were the tactics of the mother-duck, and Bashan was sincerely grateful. But he abominates those ducks who in the sleek placidity of their bourgeois-like existence, refuse to serve him as objects of the hunt, and who, whenever he comes tearing along, simply let themselves slip into the water from the stones along the banks, and then in ignoble security rock themselves before his nose, not impressed in the least by his mighty voice, and not in the least deceived, like the nervous gulls, by his theatrical lunges towards the river.

There we stand on the stones, side by side, Bashan and I, and there, two paces from us, in insolent security, the duck sways lightly upon the waves, with her bill pressed in pretentious dignity against her breast, and though stormed at by Bashan's maddened voice, absolutely undisturbed in her serenity, soberness, and common sense. She keeps rowing against the current, so that she remains approximately in about the same spot. For all that she is drawn a little downstream. Only a yard or two from her there is a whirlpool, a beautiful foaming cascade towards which she turns her conceited and upstanding tail. Bashan barks and braces

his forefeet against the stones, and inwardly
I bark with him, for I cannot forbear sharing
some of his feelings of hatred against the
duck and her cool, insolent, matter-of-fact-
ness, and so I hope that evil may overtake
her.

" Pay at least some attention to our barking," is the mental speech I hurl at her,
"and not to the rapids, so that you may be
drawn by accident into the whirlpool and
thus expose yourself to danger and discom-
fiture before our eyes."　But this angry hope
of mine is also doomed to remain unfulfilled,
for precisely at the moment when she nears
the edge of the cascade in the stream, the
duck flutters a bit and flies a few yards up-
stream and sits down in the water once more
—the shameless hussy !

I am unable to think of the vexation with
which we both contemplate the duck under
these circumstances without recalling to
mind an adventure which I shall recount at
the close.　It was attended by a certain

satisfaction for me and my companion, and yet there was something painful in it, something disturbing and confusing. Yes, it even led to a temporary chill in the relationship between Bashan and myself, and could I have foreseen this, I would rather have avoided the spot where this adventure awaited us.

It was a good distance out and downstream, and beyond the ferryman's house—there where the wilderness of the river bank approaches close to the upper road along the river. We were going along this, I with a leisurely step, and Bashan, a trifle in front of me, with an easy and somewhat lop-sided lope. He had been chasing a rabbit, or, if you prefer, had permitted himself to be chased by him. He had also routed out three or four pheasants and was now graciously minded to pay a little attention to me, so that his master might not feel utterly neglected. A small bevy of ducks with extended necks and in triangular formation

flew over the river. They were flying pretty
high and closer to the other bank than to
ours, so that we could not consider them
as game at all, so far as hunting purposes
were concerned. They flew in the direction
in which we were walking, without regarding us or even being aware of our
presence, and we too merely cast a desul-
tory and intentionally indifferent glance at
them.

It then came to pass that on the farther
bank, which was of the same steepness as
our own, a man came beating out of the
bushes. As soon as he had stepped upon the
scene of action he assumed a pose which
caused both of us, Bashan as well as myself,
to halt and to turn round and face him and
watch what he would do. He was a rather
tall, fine figure of a man, somewhat rough
and ready, so far as his externals were concerned. He had drooping moustaches and
wore puttees, a small green Alpine hat
which was well pulled over his forehead,

wide, loose trousers which were made of a kind of hard velveteen or so-called corduroy or Manchester cloth, and a jacket to match. This was behung with all kinds of belts and leather contraptions, for he carried a *rucksack* strapped to his back and a gun which also hung from a strap. Or it would be more proper to say that he had carried this, for scarcely had he come into view, than he drew the weapon towards him and leaning his cheek aslant against the butt, raised the barrel obliquely towards the heavens. He had set one be-putteed leg in front of the other, the barrel rested in the hollow of his extended left hand with the elbow bent under this—the other elbow, however, that of the right arm, the hand of which rested on the trigger, was extended very sharply towards the side. It revealed his face with squinting, aiming eye, much foreshortened and boldly exposed to the clear light of the skies.

There was something most decidedly operatic in this apparition of the man as he stood reared against the skies amidst this open-air scenery of bushes, river, and sky. Our intense and respectful regard, however, endured for only a moment —then there came the dull, flat report from over yonder—something which I had attended with great inner tension and which therefore caused me to start. A tiny jet of light, pale in the broad of day, blazed forth at the same time, and was followed by a tiny cloudlet of smoke that puffed after it. The man then inclined himself forward and once more his attitude and his action were reminiscent of the opera. And with the gun hanging from the strap, which he clutched in his right fist, he raised his face towards the skies. Something was going on up there, whither we too were now staring. There was a brief, confused scattering— the triangle of ducks flew apart, a wild, panic-stricken fluttering ensued, as when a puff of wind sets loose sails a-snapping, an attempt at a glide—as of an aeroplane—followed, then suddenly the body which had been struck became a mere inanimate object and fell swift as a stone upon the surface of the water near the opposite bank.

This was only the first half of the proceedings. But I must interrupt my narrative here in order to turn the living light of my memory upon Bashan. There are a number of coined phrases and ready-made figures of speech which I might use for describing his behaviour—current terms—terms which in most cases would be both valid and appropriate. I might say, for example, that he was thunderstruck. But this term does not please me, and I do not wish to use it. Big words, the big, well-worn words, are not very suitable for expressing the extraordinary. One may best achieve this by intensifying the small words

and forcing them to ascend to the very acme
of their meaning. So I will say no more
than that Bashan *started* at the report of the
gun and the accompanying phenomena—
and that this starting was the same as that
which is peculiar to him when confronted
with something striking, and that all this
was well known to me though it was now
elevated to the nth degree. It was a start
which flung his whole body backward,
wobbling to right and left, a start which
jerked his head in rash recoil against
his chest and which, in recovering himself, almost tore his head from his
shoulders, a start which seemed to cry
from every fibre of his being: "What,
what! *What* was that? Hold! in the
name of a hundred thousand devils! *How*
was that!"

He listened to—he regarded everything
with a kind of indignation such as extremes
of surprise are apt to cause—drank everything in, as it were, and there in his heart

of hearts these things were already existing —there, in some form or other they had always been—no matter what astounding novelties may have been sprung upon him here. Yes, whenever these things came upon him, causing him to leap to the right and the left and turn himself half around his own axis, it always seemed to me as though he were attempting to catch a glimpse of himself and inquiring : "What am I ? Who am I ? Am I really I ? " At the very moment in which the corpse of the duck fell upon the water, Bashan made a leap forward, towards the edge of the escarpment, as though he wished to go down into the river-bed and plunge himself into the water. But then he thought of the current, clamped the brakes upon this sudden impulse, grew ashamed, and once more confined his efforts to staring.

I regarded him with anxiety. After the fall of the duck, I was of the opinion that we had seen enough, and proposed that we should go on. But he had already sat himself down upon his haunches. His face, with ears erected to their utmost extent, was addressed towards the other bank, and when I said to him: "Well, Bashan, shall we go on?" he merely gave a fiirt of his head in my direction, as though one should say, not without a certain rudeness: "Please do not disturb me!" and kept on looking. And so I gave in, crossed my feet, leaned on my stick, and also went on watching to see what might now take place.

The duck—one of those very ducks which had so often in impudent security rocked itself on the water before our very noses, was driving on the water—a wreck—no one could tell which part of the bird was bow and which stern. The river is quieter here; the fall is not so great as farther up-stream. Nevertheless the carcass of the duck had been seized at once by the current, whirled about its axis and was beginning to float off.

It was clear that if our good man was not merely concerned with having made a good pot-shot and a killing, but also with a more practical purpose, then he would be obliged to put his best leg forward. This he did without losing a moment—everything happened with immense rapidity. No sooner had the duck landed in the water than the man leaped, scrambled, almost tumbled down the escarpment. He carried the shot-gun in his outstretched arm, and once more I was reminded of the opera and the romantic novel, as he went leaping down over the stage-like setting of the stone slope—like some robber chieftain or smuggler bold in a melodrama. With careful calculation he kept a little to the right in an oblique direction, for the drifting duck was being carried away from him and it was necessary to head it off. This he actually succeeded in doing with the butt of his double-barrelled gun—extending this towards his kill with his body bent far forward and with his feet in the water. He managed to halt it in its downward course. And then carefully and not without much effort he steered and piloted it against the stones with the guiding gunbutt and so drew it ashore.

The job was done and the man drew a breath of relief. He laid his gun upon the bank beside him, pulled his *rucksack* from his shoulder, stuffed his booty into it, drew the sack shut by its cords, slung it upon his shoulders. Then supporting himself on his gun as on a cane, and thus pleasantly laden, he climbed complacently up the loose stone of the slope and made for the covert.

"Well, he's got his bit of roast game for to-morrow," I thought approvingly, yet not without envy. "Come, Bashan, let's go— there's really nothing more to see." But Bashan simply stood up and turned himself once around himself, then sat down and stared after the man, even after he had already left the scene of action and vanished

among the bushes. I did not again ask him
to come along—I refused to do this as a
matter of principle. He knew where we
were living, and if he thought it reasonable to sit here still longer and stare,
after everything was over and there was
absolutely nothing more to see, well that
was his own affair. It was a long way
back, and I, for my part, was going to
return. And then at last he gave ear and
came.

During this exceedingly painful journey
homeward, Bashan refrained from all further
inclination to indulge in the sport of the
chase. He did not canter on ahead of me in
a diagonal direction as was his wont when
he was not in the right mood for trailing and
beating-up the game. He walked a little
behind me, keeping regular step and drew
down his mouth in a way which I would be
bound to notice when I turned around to
look at him. This might have been tolerated,
and I was not going to let it ruffle or upset

me—on the contrary, I was disposed to laugh
and shrug my shoulders. But then every
thirty or fifty steps he began to *yawn*, and
it was this which embittered me. It was this
shameless, wide-angle, rudely bored yawning,
accompanied by a little piping guttural
sound which clearly said : " My God ! talk
about a master ! Why, he isn't a master at
all. He's simply rotten !" This insulting
sound nearly always disturbs me, but this
time it was sufficient to shake our friendship
to its very foundations.

" Go !" I said, " go away ! Go to your
master, the man with the thunder-club,
and join up with him. He does not appear
to own a dog, and so he might give you a
job. He may need you in that business of
his. He is, of course, only a plain man in
corduroys and no particular class, but in
your eyes, no doubt, he is the finest gentle-
man in the world—a real master for you.
And so I honestly advise you to go and make
up to him—now that he has put a flea in

your ear—to keep the others company."
(Yes, I went to such extremes as this.)
"We need not inquire whether he has a
hunting permit or not, and it's quite possible
that you might get into difficulties when you
happen to be caught some fine day whilst
engaged in your shady work, but then that
is your business, and the advice which I have
given you is, as I have already remarked,
most sincere.

"The devil take your hunting," I went
on. "Did you ever bring me a single
rabbit for our table out of all those which
I permitted you to chase? Is it my fault
that you don't know how to do a quick turn
and go pounding into the gravel with your
nose like a fool at the very moment you should
be showing your agility? Or have you ever
brought me a pheasant—which would have
been just as welcome in these lean times?
And now you are—yawning! Go to that
fellow with the puttees, I say. You will
soon see whether he is the sort of man who

will scratch your throat and get you to laugh. I'd be surprised if he can laugh himself. At best, I am sure, his laugh must be a very coarse one. Perhaps you are under the impression that he would call in the aid of science and permit you to be observed in case you decide to have occult hemorrhages, perhaps you are under the delusion that once you were *his* dog, you would also have a chance to be nervous and anæmic. If so, you had better go to him. And yet it is possible that you are making a great mistake with regard to the degree of respect which this kind of master would display towards you. There are, for example, certain fine points and differences for which such gun-bearing persons have a very sharp nose, natural merits or demerits—or, to make my allusions clearer, very awkward questions regarding pedigree and breed. If I must express myself with superlative clearness, then I must say that these are things which not everybody is disposed to ignore with that delicacy and humanity to which you have been accustomed. And should your husky master—upon your first difference of opinion with him, reproach you with that goatee of yours, and call you an unpleasant name, then think of me and of the words which I am now addressing to you. . . ."

It was in such bitter irony that I spoke to Bashan as he slunk behind me on the way home, and even though I spoke inwardly and did not permit my words to be heard, so as not to appear eccentric, I am nevertheless convinced that he understood perfectly well what I meant, and that he was capable of following at least the main line of my argument. In short, the quarrel was serious, and having reached home, I purposely let the garden gate fall to close behind me and he was forced to run and clamber over the fence. Without casting a single glance behind me, I went into the house, and heard him give a squeak, as a sign that he had prodded his belly on one of the pointed pickets—something which merely produced a mocking shrug of the shoulders on my part.

But all this happened long ago—more than half a year ago. And the same thing occurred as in the matter of the clinical interim. Time and oblivion have buried it deep, and upon the floating surface of these —which constitute the base of all life,—we continue to live on. Bashan, to be sure, appeared to be rather contemplative for a few days, but he has long ago recovered his full and undiminished joy in hunting mice, pheasants, rabbits, and water-fowl, and our return home means to him merely attendance upon the next going forth. Whenever I reach my front door I turn round and face him once more, and that is the signal for him to come jumping up the steps in two great leaps in order that he may raise himself on his hind legs and stem his forepaws against the front door, so that I can pat his shoulder and say good-bye.

"To-morrow, Bashan," I remark, "we'll go out again—in case I don't have to make a trip into the big outside world." And then I hurry into the house to rid myself of my hob-nailed boots, for the soup has been served and stands smoking on the table.